Cambridge and the Evangelical Succession

Cambridge and the Evangelical Succession

Sir Marcus Loane

Copyright © Sir Marcus Loane 2007

ISBN 1-84550-244-2
ISBN 978-1-84500-244-7

10 9 8 7 6 5 4 3 2 1

First published in 1952
This edition published in 2007
by
Christian Focus Publications,
Geanies House, Fearn, Ross-shire,
IV20 1TW, Scotland

www.christianfocus.com

Cover design by Danie Van Straaten

Printed and bound by WS Bookwell, Finland

Contents

Author's Preface

THIS SERIES OF STUDIES HAS BEEN PREPARED as a companion to the similar volume called *Oxford and the Evangelical Succession*. It is designed as a study in the lives of well-known Cambridge men whose names are held in honour by all who love and serve the Evangelical Succession. My first aim has been to tell their story from records and writings, journals and letters, of their own, or of their contemporaries. Thus each study has been cast in the form of a continuous biography, but the object has been to reach a clear view of their character, their ministry, and their contribution as representative Evangelicals to the Church of England.

William Grimshaw did not perhaps carry much of Cambridge into his life or ministry; but he was linked with all the chief men of the great Movement led by Whitefield and the Wesleys. He was the first of the Pioneers of the Revival to pass away from the scene of earthly labours and to enter into the joy of his Master's presence. His life affords us a unique illustration of the way in which a churchman combined his parish duties with itinerant labours, and his friendship with Henry Venn in his early years in Yorkshire was a formative influence of great value in the life of one of the most honoured of the Evangelical Fathers.

John Berridge was much more closely linked with Cambridge, both before and after ordination. He was a resident of his college for twenty-one years, from 1734 to 1755, as student and Fellow; he was the incumbent of Everton for thirty-eight years, from 1755 to 1793, as pastor and preacher. Everton was a benefice in the gift of Clare and within easy reach of Cambridge, so that he was able to keep in touch with his Alma Mater to the close of his life. His friendship with Henry Venn of Yelling gave him direct contact with the wider circle of great Evangelical contemporaries, and his personal relations with Rowland Hill and Charles Simeon are of paramount interest in the development of Evangelical churchmanship.

Henry Venn, Charles Simeon and Henry Martyn form a definite succession; they let us see how the torch of truth and love passed from hand to hand and from age to age. Henry Venn was like a father to Charles Simeon; Simeon in turn was to Henry Martyn all that Venn had once been to him. They were all worthy sons of Cambridge; each was an honoured Fellow of his college. They were closely linked with Cambridge in the years that followed ordination as well as in the days when they read for degrees, and they left their impress on new generations in the student world who had to tread where they had once trod.

The Lady Huntingdon had been the intimate friend of Grimshaw, Berridge and Venn, and all three won their spurs in the field as itinerant preachers in an age when Order meant but little. But it was Venn who made the most direct impact upon Simeon and Martyn, and all three made their mark in the world as deliberate churchmen in an age when Order came to matter. They proved themselves worthy heirs of the great Reformation heroes such as Bilney and Tyndale and Ridley and Cranmer, who had sought light and found it at Cambridge in the sixteenth century. And the Succession is still unbroken; the light which they kindled must not go out.

I owe a very warm debt of gratitude to the Right Reverend Hugh Gough, Bishop of Barking, himself a Cambridge man, who has so kindly written the Foreword for these studies. It is my great desire that the pages which now follow will not only do full honour to the great Cambridge Evangelicals, but will also help us to catch afresh that deep inspiration from on high which made them great in love and service for their Lord and Saviour.

'He did his utmost for God. Seldom had the sun ever run half his daily course before this minister had once or oftener declared the testimony of the Lord, which enlightens the eyes of the mind and rejoices the hearts of the poor. All intent on this work, every day had its destined labours of love, morning and evening, to fill up. Labours so great, that it is almost incredible to tell how many hours of the twenty-four were constantly employed in instructing those who dwelt in his parish or in neighbouring places. Never was any sordid child of this world more engrossed by the love of money and more laborious in heaping it up, than (William Grimshaw) in teaching and preaching the Kingdom of God!'

Henry Venn: Funeral Sermon (cf. Cragg, Grimshaw of Haworth, p. 106)

1

William Grimshaw
1708-63

William Grimshaw was born in the little village of Brindle on 3 September 1708, and he grew up in the Lancashire countryside not far from the three new seats of manufacture at Preston, Chorley and Blackburn. Very meagre is the stock of detailed information which has come down to us even of his life as a whole, and the records of his early days are barest of all. His life stretched from the last years of Queen Anne to the first years of King George III. He lived through the stirring days of the first Jacobite Rebellion in the reign of George I before he had reached his teens; he passed through the thrilling days of the last Jacobite Rebellion in the reign of George II as a beneficed clergyman in the Church of England. But he did not figure in the public eye as a man of political or literary talent in that age of cultured unrest, and the faith he proclaimed was held in dire contempt by the best known names in fashionable society. Grimshaw did not even share the fame of men like Whitefield and the Wesleys, for he never gave up his post as a settled curate with settled duties to perform. He was content to live and die in a Yorkshire parish, to move in the narrow orbit of his own bleak country; he did indeed travel widely in and beyond his own parish all through the North, but he hardly ever went South and was virtually unknown to the crowds in London. Within his own orbit, he was a star of the first magnitude; but his light was not shed over the length and breadth of the whole land. He kept no private journal, and wrote no *magnum opus*; but his name and worth flash through the Lives and Letters of his great contemporaries, and it is from quarries such as these that we must gather our scant materials for the study of his character and his ministry.

We know nothing of his home-life or his parents, but they must have striven to give the lad the best education which small means could command. He went to the Grammar School at Blackburn, and passed on from there to one at Heskin. We can not tell how far he was moved by religious sentiment, but his proficiency led his parents to send him on to read for Orders at Cambridge. Thus in 1726, at the age of eighteen, he was entered as a student at Christ's College, and there embarked on his studies for the customary degree. This was three years before Wesley and his friends at Oxford began to meet weekly for the study of the New Testament in Greek; but there was no Holy Club nor Christian Fellowship within the four walls of any Cambridge College in that cold year of grace. Two hundred years before, in the 1520's, Cambridge was in the lead in the search for light and reality; it had been the centre where Barnes and Frith, Bilney and Cranmer, Coverdale and Latimer, had read and prayed over the Greek Text brought out by Erasmus. Cambridge had forged the links in the moral armour of men like these who were to lay down life and all for Christ and the gospel; but the lapse of those two hundred years since Tyndale had grown in his grasp of God's Word or since Ridley had stored up his mind with its text, had left Cambridge steeped in darkness almost as dense as that of the long mediaeval night. Grimshaw spent his four or five years in Christ's, and took his Arts degree in the easy fashion which then prevailed; but those valuable years passed away without light or blessing for mind or heart in the grace and mercy of God. He got no good for his own soul, and did little else but learn to drink and swear like the rest of the world.

The year 1731 was marked by his ordination to the Diaconate, and he became curate to the chapel at Littleborough in the Parish of Rochdale in Lancashire. He seems to have been roused by his ordination to a fleeting sense of the real solemnity of his office, but he entered on his work in desperate ignorance of its duties and its demands. The Parish of Rochdale had a meeting where a group of godly minded men and women met for prayer and Bible study, and he gladly joined them; he was also given a few books to which in later years he was glad to turn for light and comfort. But his stay in Rochdale was all too short, for in the self-same year he was transferred to a curacy at Todmorden. This was a small chapelry in the patronage of his vicar; it lay in the heart of the moors, in a wild but romantic valley between Rochdale and Leeds. Eleven crucial years were to be spent in this lonely region, years which were to mark the cross-roads in his immortal pilgrimage. But the lonely curate slipped back for a time with all speed into the old Cambridge habits, and soon became the easy companion of easy men. He knew the dark side of human nature, not as a man who had formed some confused idea of a far-off country with the aid of a map, but as one who had long lived in the land and had explored it in detail.[1] He would hunt and fish and play cards in the free style of his fellow clergy with their neighbours, and was content to dismiss his duties when he had said prayers twice and had read a single sermon on the Lord's Day. He knew nothing aright as to the state of his own soul, or the way to do good to the souls of others. He told Mary Scholefield of Calf Lee who came to ask his advice: 'Put away these gloomy thoughts; go into merry company; divert yourself; and all will be well at last.'[2] But deep down in his heart he knew that all was not so well as it might seem; and he tried to refrain from gross swearing when not in suitable company, while he always took care to sleep off a drunken stupor before he appeared in public.

But a change was at hand, and we can still piece together the few facts which have come down to us. The year 1734 saw him for the first time under concern for his own soul and the souls of others, and a change crept over his life and its mode of conduct. His cards were put away, and he forsook the lure of the river and the call of the chase. He set out to visit the homes of his people, urging them to bethink themselves of the solemn claims of eternity. He gave himself up to seek the Face of God on his knees in prayer four times each day, and this was a habit, so we learn from Henry Venn, which he still maintained at the close of his life. But all this was at best no more than an interim condition; he was in a kind of spiritual twilight. He was weighed down by the burden of guilt, but as yet knew nothing of the comfort of grace; his eyes had been opened to see God as holy, but not to see Him as One who loves to forgive. He had few books to guide him, and no friends to speak with him; he felt that his life was useless, yet he knew not where to turn for help or counsel. He was groping for light like a man who was lost, and this struggle to find the way was to last for some years. He had begun to preach in a strain of energetic condemnation of sin, and his flock was urged to flee from the wrath to come; but his sermons remained chill and cheerless, for he could not point them to One who was mighty to save. He was in fact a blind leader of the blind, and his own state of mind is clearly disclosed in his reply to a woman who came to him in real distress of soul: 'I cannot tell what to say to you, Susan,' he said, 'for I am in the same state myself; but to despair of the mercy of God would be worse than all.'[3]

But there were deep waters through which he had to pass before he could ground his feet on the solid rock of peace and certainty. The year 1734 had seen his wedding with a widow who had been a Lockwood from Ewood Hall as well as the great change in his manner of life, and the next five years of married bliss were years of truest love and home life. A son and a daughter were born to fill that home with their gladsome laughter; and then, his wife fell ill and died. On November 1, 1739 she was buried beneath the fells in the little church at Luddenden, and her grave lay within sound of the soft plash of the stream as it flowed on its way to the Calder. Grimshaw had loved his wife dearly, and her death came as a great shock to him; he would visit Ewood as a mourner all through the years that were yet to follow, and there at last he was himself to be buried. But the meantime left him as a desolate widower with two little children, his chief earthly comfort gone, and himself as yet without the comfort of heaven. His heart was now racked with a new kind of anguish, and all his thirst for peace with God took on a fresh intensity. For three more years he was still to remain in the twilight shadows, walking alone in the gloom of his own feelings; but he clung to the staff of prayer and the study of the Scriptures, and in due time the clear light of truth was to dawn. At length he turned back to the books which he had been given while at Rochdale, and two volumes of strong Puritan instruction helped to draw him to God. Brooks brought home to him a stronger sense of his own guilt and wretchedness; Owen put his feet on the track which led him out into the glad sunshine of mercy. Eight years had passed by since his first awakening, but while the year 1742 was yet green, the last scales dropped from his eyes.

Grimshaw had passed out of darkness into the warm sweet light of the gospel without aid from any human quarter; his change of heart was quite independent of the mighty movement which was then on foot in London and the south of England. He had once heard someone preach a sermon on the Divine Rescue by means of faith alone, and he had thought it a Romish kind of doctrine; but faith had now come to life in his own soul and proclaimed peace to his heart. Thus long before he came into contact with men like John Wesley and George Whitefield, he had arrived at the same great doctrinal conclusions on the twin themes of the Grace of God and the Guilt of Man; and this independent discovery of truth doubtless helped to convince him that there was as much freedom for the preaching of the gospel as he needed within the pale of the Church of England. Thus he returned to his labours with all that energy and devotion which were soon known as the hall marks of an Evangelical; like a traveller who had mistaken his way, he now tried to double his speed on the right road to make up for lost time. 'I was now willing', he told Venn, 'to renounce myself, every degree of fancied merit and ability, and to embrace Christ as my all in all. O what light and comfort did I enjoy in my own soul, and what a taste of the pardoning love of God!'[4] He once declared that it was as though God had drawn his old Bible up to heaven, and had let down a new version of the Scriptures—such a flood of light now seemed to stream down on the sacred page where all had been dark before. He soon sought out Mary Scholefield, and tried to set her right. 'O Mary,' he said, 'what a blind leader of the blind was I, when I came to take off thy burden by exhorting thee to live in pleasure, and to follow the vain amusements of the world!'[5] He was still a mighty huntsman, but the prey he stalked was the souls of men; and his ministry in the Vale of Todmorden was now to be exchanged for the prime scene of his earthly labours.

In May 1742 Grimshaw moved to Haworth, a little Yorkshire chapelry within the huge Parish of Bradford, 'one of those obscure places which like the fishing towns in Galilee...owe all their celebrity to the gospel'.[6] It stands on the line of hills which run down from the Lakes in the north to the Peak of Derbyshire, hills which divide the West Riding from the County of Lancashire. The whole traverse of this country is bleak, rugged, desolate, and weather-beaten, and the moors in the north are as wild and as steep as the Scottish Highlands. The village of Haworth lies at the top of the roughest stretch of the West Riding, about four miles from the town of Keighley and eight miles from Bradford; it was well known as a rough and lawless village on the fringe of wild and lonely moorland, cut off from the crowded cities by mile after mile of rolling heather. It was described in Domesday Book as desolate and waste, and time had done little to mend this grim aspect of things. It was a cold, lean, grey village, built of brown stone, quite bare of trees, approached by a steep rise from Hebden Bridge and the town of Keighley. In 1820 Patrick Bronte and his family came to reside in the Vicarage, and this has made Haworth famous in the annals of our literature. In 1850 Herschel Babbage drew up a long report for the Board of Health which makes it clear that Haworth was still backward in the extreme. The death rate per annum was as high as that in the worst parts of London, and two-fifths of those who died were children less than six years of age. The roads were in dreadful need of repair, and there was no proper sanitation; beer was consumed in an alarming proportion, and the churchyard was ringed with alehouses. Things must have been worse one hundred years before when Grimshaw went to Haworth; a land of less promise could not easily be imagined.

Grimshaw had not only come to one of the most lonely and most dreary spots in England; he had also come to a cure of souls who were as low in things spiritual as in all things material. The church had been vacant for three years past, and a scandal before that had ended in the suspension of the incumbent from his Orders. The whole village had lapsed into heathen ways of life and outlook, and there were few who would even attend the church. Many of the people in and out of Haworth were small independent workmen who farmed a few acres of land, and combed or wove at home for the new worsted industry. They would divide their time between the sheep on the open moorland, and their work in little low rooms where they heated their combs over red-hot charcoals. They were craftsmen proud of their skill, but dead to all the more wholesome pursuits of mind and soul. Sunday was the market day in Bradford, and those who were not at market would play football out on the moors. Fair time was an open season of riot and debauchery, and horse-races on the moors just beyond Haworth brought a great trade to the inns and ale houses. Every wedding had its entertainment in the form of foot-races, when the near-naked runners were a scandal to all decent strangers. Every funeral had its feast, or 'arvill', when the mourners met in drunken orgies and broke up at length in stand-to battles.[7] Such was the field and such the flock to which Grimshaw had come; the bleak and barren face of the country was a fitting emblem of the wild state of its people who had little more real care for God than the sheep out on the moors. Grimshaw told John Newton in long after years that when he came to Haworth he could ride for a full half-day, east, west, north, south, and not meet a single godly soul, nor even hear tell of one.[8] The tide was ebb and low when he arrived, but he was not dismayed; he was to see it turn at length, and roll in with the full force of omnipotent blessing.

The first aspect of things was dark enough. 'Thick-thewed, and slow of speech, and sullenly suspicious of a stranger, gruff, and stubborn, and hating restraint, his little flock greeted him with their favourite motto: Keep thyseln to thyseln!'[9] But that aspect soon began to alter, for the Haworth townsfolk found that their new parson was a man as brawny, as fearless, and as strong-willed as they were themselves.[10] Grimshaw at once began to preach in the plainest spirit to his rough and reckless hearers, and he followed up his sermons with house-to-house visitation. He would not let difficulties daunt him; he met them with a bold unorthodox approach which swept all barriers aside. Sunday football and the market clamour on the Lord's Day were soon brought to an end: the ale houses were soon to stand empty in the hour of worship, and woe betide the man who would dare to absent himself from church! There was preaching twice a Sunday, at the service after lunch as well as in the morning; and when people complained that their 'poor and foul cloaths' made it impossible for them to come to church, he arranged a lecture for them in the evening with prayers in his own house.[11] He rode the bounds of his parish with an eye that was wide open for those that were astray, and they soon found that he thought no labour too great for their recovery. They found also that his self-denial was as great as his zeal for their souls, for he was as kind to them in things temporal as he was firm with them in things eternal. He was willing to preach in a quarry, by the roadside, in a room, in a barn; many a quaint scene might have been observed in the narrow hedgerows. He would accost men as to the state of their souls, and would ask them if they went wont to pray; when the answer was yes, he would bid them kneel down and let him hear. It was well said that he would 'rive them from horseback to make them pray!'[12]

Grimshaw had found a field of work so wide that it was to fill his hands all through the one-and-twenty years of life that remained, but the energy and the diligence with which he set out to redeem the time have seldom been equalled. One of the first problems which he had to solve was how to provide for four scattered hamlets in his parish; if the people were too far off to come in to Haworth, he must needs go out to farm or cottage and meet them there. This led to a visit to each hamlet three times a month, and these cottage meetings were in full swing within his first twelve months. Thus he embarked on an itinerant life in his own parish, and was preaching no less than twelve sermons a month in the village kitchens for a number of years before he met Whitefield or the Wesleys. We cannot feel surprised that a new breath of life and zeal began to fan the whole district; many began to think about their souls who had never concerned themselves before. The first twelve months saw the first signs of the coming harvest, and in 1755 he was able to write of that early seed-time back in 1742 with thankful joy:

> In that year, our dear Lord was pleased to visit my parish. A few souls were affected under the Word, brought to see their lost estate by nature, and to experience peace through faith in the blood of Jesus. My church began to be crowded, in so much that many were obliged to stand out of doors.[13]

And those early days saw other scenes, such as the Wesleys had sometimes seen; people fell like slaked lime under a sense of their guilt and the wrath of God. They would rend the air with cries of anguish; tears would course down their cheeks as they wept with remorse. Haworth was now the scene of a movement by the Spirit of God in which converts were soon to be reckoned, not in ones or in twos, but in scores if not in hundreds. Such scenes were new to the Church of England, which had not been troubled by the excessive popularity of its preachers since the days of Richard Baxter.

Various anecdotes grew up round the name of Grimshaw which still help to throw a broad beam of light on the man and his ministry. He was nothing if not direct both in rebuke and in appeal; friends as well as strangers came in for their full share of such candid address. Thus he once heard Whitefield tell his people that they enjoyed such great blessings in the church at Haworth that there was less need for him to say much to them. Grimshaw sprang to his feet, and spoke out with stern voice: 'Oh, sir! For God's sake, do not speak so! I pray you, do not flatter them! I fear the greater part of them are going to hell with their eyes open!'[14] It was zeal like this that led him to go the round of wakes and fairs, in search of the wilder and more wayward of his parishioners. He found that boys from the village used to meet out on the moors on Sunday mornings in the summer for card-playing and other games, and he resolved to dress up in disguise in an attempt to put an end to the practice. He went out in the garb of an old woman, and made his way into their midst without exciting suspicion; then he peeled off his garments, and took down their names while they stood dumb with surprise. He told them to come and see him at a set time, and they came just as if they had been served with a warrant; he knelt down in their midst, and poured out his desires in prayer. Then he gave them such a lecture as they never forgot, and the custom was clean broken.[15] Grimshaw also set out to quash the horse-races, but could make no headway in his appeals to the sponsors; at last he made it known that he would talk no more with man, but would address himself to God. Race-time came round once more, and the crowds poured into Haworth for the satanic carnival of drink and riot; but thick clouds spread over the sky, and for three days there was such a torrent of rain that no man nor beast could broach the race-track. It was soon said that old Grimshaw had put a stop to the races, and the fact was that his prayers had washed them out once and for all.[16]

Legends like these tell a tale which we ought not to ignore; the man of whom they speak was no common country parson. When sayings and doings such as these are treasured up and handed down from age to age, it is clear that they enshrine someone who was out of the ordinary mould. The most famous story of all is told on the authority of John Newton; it paints his zeal against Sunday desecration with a background which we love to recall with a sense of pleasant humour. There were four ale houses within a stone's throw of the church, and he knew that the men of the parish were more often there than in their place for worship. Thus he himself would leave the church during the Psalm prior to the sermon, and would go out to round up the idlers at street corners or in the ale houses. One of the six bylaws for the town of Kidderminster in the days of Baxter required the churchwardens to leave the church as soon as the Second Lesson was read, and to search the taverns for absentees and loiterers.[17] Grimshaw liked to announce Psalm 119 so as to give him enough time to fetch them all in, and one old tradition says that he was wont to arm himself with a horse-whip for the purpose![18] Newton does not mention this fact, and it may be apocryphal; but he relates at least one incident which goes far to bear the point out. A friend of his happened to pass one of the inns at the crucial hour one Sunday morning, and was startled to see a group of men making the most rapid exit from its windows. Some were jumping down from a sash close to the ground; some were leaping over a low wall just beyond. He thought that the inn was on fire, and he began to ask questions in some alarm; but he was told that the fuss was due to the fact that they had caught sight of Grimshaw on his way to drive them from the tavern to the service. They had a more wholesome fear of Grimshaw's whip than they had for the devil himself, and his reproofs were so mild and yet so final that the stoutest sinner could not well resist him.[19]

His conduct of public worship in the church at Haworth was as remarkable as his preaching; nothing that was merely formal would he suffer for one moment. Reality was the key-note of the service, as of all that he did; there was a life and fire about the man, an earnestness of spirit and reverence of manner, which could hardly fail to strike and arrest. His eye would sweep the whole congregation before the prayers began, and prompt rebuke would crush the man who was lounging forward when he ought to have been down on his knees.[20] The Prayer Book came to life as his voice rose and fell, and the lectern was as stirring as the pulpit. He would read the Lessons, with a pause to translate all that was hard into plain broad Yorkshire or to open up the meaning with his homely comments. He would sometimes engage in extempore prayer after the Third Collect, and his soul used to be carried out with that deep fervour which told of a very close walk with God. While the congregation sang the last Psalm before the time for the sermon, his robes were laid aside and he went out to round up the stragglers. The Black Bull would soon be emptied, and then he would return to take his place in an old-fashioned three-decker pulpit. His prayer seemed to lay siege to the very Throne of Glory, and he would not let go until he was sure that God had heard and blessed him. One hearer observed that in prayer 'he excelled most men I have ever heard'.[21] Another listener declared: 'His voice in prayer seemed to me as it had been the voice of an angel.'[22] It was said that 'he was at times like a man with his feet on earth, and his soul in heaven'.[23] Then would come the sermon on such a text as would set forth the Cross of Christ, and there were times when he would preach for two full hours at least.[24] But the crowded church would listen from first to last, while tears ran down many a cheek; and men seldom thought him too long, for they went home like those who had heard for eternity.[25]

Grimshaw's sermons were blunt and bold, 'hale with uncompromising dogma, yet full of racy thrusts and quiet dry humour' such as Yorkshire hearers love most.[26] He was a born orator, and spoke with the greatest facility; but he was first and last a plain messenger, whose one aim was to bring home the truth to heart and conscience. He would not speak in the accents of his Cambridge training to men who stood in need of the strongest broadside in their own tongue; he felt compelled to preach 'in the same style as that in which Albert Durer painted'.[27] It was his plan to preach with a constant variety of thought and phrase, and John Newton's comments on this aspect of his sermons are still worth calm recognition. He chose 'market language' which was within the range of the dullest understanding, and his sermons were packed with quaint sayings and crisp proverbs.[28] He had a flair for the common things of life, for homely illustrations which would capture the most careless of his hearers and would focus their thoughts on the things that are eternal. There were moments perhaps when his homely forms of speech were scarcely dignified, but his market language was on the whole strikingly impressive. 'If you perish', he would cry, 'you shall perish with the sound of the gospel in your lugs!'[29] His aim was to preach man down and to preach Christ up, and the very freshness of his preaching made men willing to walk twenty miles to hear him.[30] There were hundreds as a result who learnt to fear Hell and the wrath of God, though they never really felt the love of heaven; there were hundreds who were restrained from the open practice of sin, though they never rightly sought for mercy. But the real fruit of such preaching was to be seen, not in the field of such restraint where no moral weed found it sweet to thrive, but in the great harvest of souls which was reaped both in and beyond the Parish of Haworth.

He took great care of the fabric as well as the worship of the church at Haworth. If he made his service a true model of all that the Prayer Book Service ought to be in life and reality, he was also at pains to see that the church was furnished with a becoming dignity. In 1742 a new font was consecrated, and a new three-decker pulpit was set up in the church. On the sounding-board he inscribed his two favourite texts: 'For I determined not to know anything among you save Jesus Christ and Him crucified'

(1 Cor. 2: 2), and 'For to me to live is Christ, and to die is gain' (Phil. 1 : 21). He found that the parish was used to one sermon only on the Lord's Day, and he at once began to preach twice each Sunday. He found that the Communion Service was not celebrated more than six times a year, and he tried to arrange for a monthly Sacrament. In June 1743 there were but 326 families in the parish, and of these only three were Dissenters from the Church of England. There were none of his churchgoers who had not been baptized, but there were 400 who were ready to be confirmed.[31] In 1743 there was one small school for forty children;[32] in 1750 two new flagons were set apart for use at the Sacrament.[33] His first twelve months had seen the church packed with hearers, and he induced the trustees to provide for more accommodation; but they stipulated that there should be no tax or rate for this purpose, and that he should expect nothing but their voluntary contributions.[34] His own entry in the General Register began: 'We…desire to enlarge the church for the more open and orderly attendance of public worship of Almighty God, wherein we are greatly interrupted and disturbed by outcomers from divers parishes.' Here the entry broke off as though he thought that his remark on those who came from a distance was not tactful enough, and he began again: '… wherein we are in the said church greatly interrupted and disturbed by too exceeding a congregation of people.' Neighbour clergy could not object to that, and the work was carried on for twelve years, from 1743 till 1755, when at last the church stood new and complete.[35]

It is absurd to talk as though Grimshaw were not a true churchman. In June 1743 the Visitation Returns for Archbishop Herring show that it was his rule to catechize from Easter to Whitsun each year, and his only complaint was that people were not particular to send both their children and their servants for the purpose.[36] In August 1747 he informed John Wesley that it was his custom to expound the Articles and Homilies each year, and he urged his people in and out of season to hold fast by the Means of Grace.[37] He thought that long neglect of the Articles was the main cause of all dissent, and that men would never have left the Church had they been read and their doctrines enforced. He once said that an old clergyman of his acquaintance was asked by his curate if he might read from the Homilies, but the answer was No! 'For if you should do so, the whole congregation would turn Methodist!'[38] In 1755 he wrote to Charles Wesley:

> I am determined to live and die a member and a minister of the Church of England; for although I can by no means endure the doctrines and deportment of the clergy in general, yet I have no reason to quarrel with our Church. Her Articles, Homilies, Catechism, and Liturgy, for the main, are orthodox and good.[39]

This was plain speech from one who sat loose to many a church custom in his wider witness, but he never faltered in this belief. In 1760 he wrote again to Charles Wesley, and spoke his mind as plainly as ever.

> I see nothing so materially amiss in the Liturgy or the Church constitution as to disturb my conscience or justify my separation. No; where shall I go to mend myself? I believe the Church of England to be the soundest, purest, and most apostolical national Christian Church in the world; therefore I can in good conscience, as I am determined, God willing, to do, live and die in her.[40]

Grimshaw's preaching fame soon spread far beyond Haworth, and there were scores, if not hundreds, who came regularly to hear him from beyond his own parish borders. It was common for the clergy to preach only at the morning service, and to catechize in the afternoon; but those who had a mind for truth preferred to go to a distant church like Haworth rather than miss out a second sermon. Strangers from the nearby towns of Yorkshire would ride over on the Sunday morning, and as many as a hundred would dine at the village inns before the afternoon service.[41] Then they asked him to come and preach at small cottage meetings in their own towns, and they promised him a hearty welcome if he would step outside his own parish.

He knew that there were scores of these hamlets all through the north where there was no resident minister and where the church was bare and cold and dead. He had begun the twelve cottage meetings each month in the scattered hamlets of his own home parish; but this was a call from beyond which he could not refuse. Thus he would mount his horse and ride over the moors where the only tracks were pony tracks which climbed up and down the steep defiles from village to village, long and lonely trails which few would use save the Scottish packman or the West Riding clothier. Joseph Williams heard in 1747 from the landlord at Colne that he was then preaching in barns or homes almost daily,[42] and Charles Wesley heard that self-same year that he was preaching as far away as East Lancashire.[43] Thus he was an itinerant beyond his own parish before he had ever met George Whitefield or the Wesleys, and he no more derived his views from them than did St. Paul from the Twelve in Jerusalem. He had early learnt to group his converts in small societies, and a letter to John Gillies describes just how the work had grown: 'After a season, I joined people such as were truly seeking or had found the Lord in society for meetings and exercises; these meetings are held once a week…consisting of about ten or twelve members each.'[44]

Grimshaw knew that all these extra-parochial labours were not likely to be looked on with much favour; but he argued that his offence was no more than that of a man who was irregular for the love of souls, while there were still scores of pluralist clergymen who were irregular for love of the world.[45] So too Berridge was to plead in his own defence when asked by his bishop for an account of his preaching outside his own parish: 'Why, my Lord, I see many parsons playing at bowls and going a-hunting out of their own parishes, yet they meet with no reproofs; why should I be blamed more than they?'[46] The real state of affairs in the Archdiocese of York bore out these claims with all too much accuracy. In 1743 Archbishop Herring held a Visitation which still reveals the facts with stark rudeness. Replies came in from 836 parishes, in 393 of which there was no resident incumbent.

There were 711 clergy, of whom no less than 335 were pluralists. All this meant that there were many churches which could not be served twice on the Lord's Day, and the number which did have two Sunday ministrations all the year round was less than half by far. There were only seventy-two parish churches which had monthly celebrations of the Communion Service; and 193 which tried to arrange a two-monthly celebration; there were 363 which had a quarterly Sacrament, while 208 were even less frequent.[47] In 1761 Archbishop Drummond told Dr Conyers Middleton: 'Were you to inculcate the morality of Socrates, it would do more good than canting about the New Birth.'[48] There was a great famine in that land, and Grimshaw went out to meet it boldly with the Bread of Life.

Thus he began the long career which was to know no rest while life remained, 'preaching early and late with great success'; so ran the note in the General Register of the Church at Haworth after his death.[49] The bounds of his activity widened from his parish to a circuit which in time spread over four large counties, and he was known throughout Yorkshire and Cheshire, Derbyshire and Lancashire. He soon had two weekly rounds as well as his own parish meetings, and, with occasional variations, he kept to these circuits for years. One of these he pleasantly called his lazy or idle week, because he seldom preached more than twelve or fourteen times; but the other was his busy or working week, because he would preach from twenty to thirty times![50] It must be borne in mind that these cottage meetings and street preachings were not held in church hours, and that to the end he urged his hearers to be regular at the Sacraments of the Church of England.[51] We cannot now trace the extent of his labours in its detail, but the annals of his brethren in the same work record the names of towns in which he used to preach. We hear of him in the remote Yorkshire dales, and as far north as Osmotherley and Barnard Castle; we hear of him in the crowded city streets, and as far south as Halifax and Manchester. Thus he travelled hundreds of miles, year in, year out, content with the humblest fare and meanest quarters, oft-times weary, sometimes lonely, but happy in communion with God and ardent in compassion for souls. 'Witness ye moors and mountains,' cried Henry Venn after his death, 'how often he was in perils by the way!...Witness ye stormy rains and piercing colds,...how many seasons he exposed himself to your inclemencies if by any means he might save some!'[52]

It is perhaps hard to conceive how he kept this up for twenty long years without being stopped by an archdeacon, if not the archbishop. He was strongly opposed by the clergy; he was sometimes attacked by the people. Nevertheless, be the cause what it may, he was never forced to leave off; the hand of God was with him, and strengthened him to the end. He was obliged to pledge himself not to preach in any place of worship licensed for the cause of Dissent, but he affirmed that he would preach abroad elsewhere as long as there were souls for whom none seemed to care. In 1749 he was accused before His Grace of York as one who went preaching outside his own parish, but the interview was well overruled. The racy dialogue began with the question: 'How many communicants had you when you first came to Haworth?' And he said: 'Twelve, my Lord.' Then he was asked how many he had now, and he replied: 'In the winter, from three to four hundred; and in the summer, near twelve hundred.' He had raised the number from twelve to twelve hundred; what more was there to say? 'We cannot find fault with Mr Grimshaw,' was the verdict, 'when he is instrumental in bringing so many persons to the Lord's Table.'[53] But a further report led the worthy prelate down to Haworth for a Sunday Confirmation, and the irate clergy came to watch this personal encounter. His Grace told him that he had heard some strange reports of his activities, and asked him to preach in two hours' time from a text which he then named for the discourse. Grimshaw thought that he was to be turned out of his parish, and was ready to pack up his saddle-bags and join John Wesley; but he took the pulpit forthwith, and then engaged in prayer with such fervour that the people, and the clergy, and the Archbishop himself, were moved to tears. When the service came to a close, His Grace of

York took him by the hand and said with tremulous voice in the hearing of all: 'I would to God that all the clergy in my diocese were like this good man!'[54]

The West Riding was the field of action for yet another pioneer of the gospel in the early 'forties; this was the Rev. Benjamin Ingham, Methodist and Moravian, an erstwhile student at Oxford. He was born in Yorkshire in 1712, and became a member of Queens' College in 1730. Four years later, in 1734, he joined Wesley and his friends in the Holy Club, but in spite of prayers and fasts and discipline, his heart was far from peace with God. In June 1735 he was ordained in the Church of England, and at once joined the two Wesleys in their mission to Georgia. He was deeply impressed by the Moravian missionaries who were also on their way to America, but he was still seeking to be saved by his own merits rather than by simple faith in Jesus. In 1737 he went home to England to get recruits for the mission, but the return of John Wesley a month or two later marked the collapse of that venture. Ingham, like the Wesleys, was led ere long to trust in Christ alone for grace and salvation, and a new fire began to burn in their yielded spirits. In June 1738 Ingham and John Wesley set out on a visit to Count Zinzendorf at the Wetterau and the Brethren further south at Hernhutt. In 1739 he was back in England, and he made his home in Yorkshire. He soon began to preach both in church and chapel, and many were led to Christ as their Saviour. But in June he was barred from all pulpits in the Province of York, and thus found himself in Yorkshire in the same plight as Wesley in London. Both were ordained in the Church of England, and both longed to preach the gospel; but they were shut out of church and pulpit, and they took to village greens and public streets, fields and barns. By the year 1740 Ingham had formed forty societies for his converts, and by 1742 he had more than fifty of these societies all over Yorkshire and Lancashire.

It would seem that Ingham first came into touch with Grimshaw during the year 1743, and the two men soon found that their hearts beat as one. Ingham had employed lay preachers like

John Nelson in his societies for the last two years, and he was working freely both with the Methodists and the Moravians; it was he who first led Grimshaw to perceive the value of lay preachers when he put him in touch with a layman by the name of William Darney. Grimshaw at first was loath to take him up, but he could not deny the force of his preaching. As a result, it was not long before he might be seen giving out hymns, not to mention leading in prayer, at the layman's meetings, and word ran round that 'Mad Grimshaw' had become Scotch Will's Clerk![55] It was a step which he never learned to regret, and in course of time he began to send laymen out on his own account. He was always glad to listen to an unlettered lay-preacher who might be far inferior to himself. 'Your sermons', he once remarked to a layman, 'are worth a hundred of mine.'[56] Meanwhile Ingham's societies grew to upwards of sixty in number, and they were well scattered over all the northern counties of the Kingdom. Meetings for his preachers were held from time to time, and each circuit was mapped out in detail. 'Grimshaw invariably attended these meetings and always preached, never troubling himself to ask the consent of the minister of the parish or caring whether he liked it or not.'[57] He joined Ingham wholeheartedly in his societies, and he laboured unweariedly to spread the glad tidings through his circuit. Once or twice in each year he would travel the round and preach for his friend in all the centres which had been established. But this friendship had a direct bearing on the development of Grimshaw's ministry in more senses than one; it was, under God, the means of making him known to the leading men in the great revival of the age.

The Lady Selina Shirley was born within four years of John Wesley, on August 24, 1707, and she lived to survive him by a few short weeks before her death on June 17, 1791. She was brought up in ways of true culture and piety, and she set her heart from childhood on the pursuit of God and of glory. In June 1728 she was married to the ninth Earl of Huntingdon, and this union of the Houses of Shirley and Hastings marked the union of two of the oldest and most famous Houses in the English peerage. Her two sisters-in-law, Lady Betty and Lady Margaret, were women of singular excellence, and all three gave themselves up to works of charity in the name of religion. But the time came when her sisters-in-law were in Yorkshire on a visit to their aunt, the Lady Betty Hastings of Ledstone Hall, and news of the preaching of the Yorkshire evangelists came to their ears. The two ladies happened to hear Ingham, who was on a visit to a nearby parish, and the result was an invitation for him to preach in Ledstone Church. He was soon a regular visitor at the Hall, and Lady Margaret drank from the streams of life and truth. In December 1739 their aunt died, and Ledstone Hall passed into its new ownership by the Earl of Huntingdon. His two sisters came to reside with him at the family residence of Donnington Hall, and their loving witness was soon the means by which the Lord touched and opened the eyes of the Countess. In a conversation with Lady Margaret, she was deeply impressed by the simple statement that 'since she had known and believed in the Lord Jesus Christ for life and salvation, she had been as happy as an angel'.[58] This remark came back to her in an illness which soon threatened her life, and she in turn was able to trust in Christ and Christ alone for life and salvation.

As the daughter of one earl and wife of another, she was now to prove that:

> Kind hearts are more than coronets,
> And simple faith than Norman blood.[59]

For when the head that wears a coronet goes with a heart absorbed in love to God and man, and when one of ancient House is inspired by lofty faith, then grace transcends human rank, and mortal worth is lost in divine nobility. Jesus, the Sun of Righteousness, had shone in on her soul with full meridian glory, and her life was thenceforth to be spent for Christ as her All in all. But the future did not unfold all at once, and the next development took place in Yorkshire. In November 1741

Lady Margaret and Benjamin Ingham were married; she was twelve years older and of a much higher rank in society, but it was a union of deep and lasting love. Then in 1743 the Earl and Countess of Huntingdon travelled north to Ledstone Hall, on their first visit since the death of Lady Betty, and the Inghams soon brought Grimshaw over as a guest to the Hall. There was preaching twice a day for some days, and the crowds who flocked from a great distance were numbered in thousands. The Earl and his noble Lady now began to visit Ledstone Hall each summer, and a special round of preaching in the church or in the open air was always a part of their programme. Grimshaw was a well-known figure at these seasons, and he quickly became a great favourite with Lady Huntingdon. In October 1746 the Earl's death left her a widow, and she began to fill up her life with the work of Christ's Kingdom. She made William Romaine and George Whitefield her two chaplains, and she threw open her home at Chelsea to the preaching of the gospel. She had access to the highest circles in the Kingdom, and no hostess in all London could outmatch her drawing-room with a more brilliant conclave of guests. Grimshaw never came to London nor preached in her house at Chelsea, but her journeys north to Ledstone Hall and Yorkshire always brought him to her side.

The year 1742 saw John Wesley on his first journey as far as Yorkshire, but it was not until 1746 that Grimshaw met either of the brothers. Their names must have become known to him through Ingham, and he gladly welcomed them when the West Riding was drawn into their wide orbit. In 1746 Charles Wesley travelled north through Haworth, and found Grimshaw ill with fever but 'full of triumphant love';[60] in 1747 John Wesley paid two visits to the county, and preached to 'a numerous congregation' at Haworth.[61] It is clear that Grimshaw stood in with the Wesleys from this time on; he was at one with them in all their plans, and their zeal was a true match for his own. He followed John's visit in May by a preaching tour of all the chapels in Will Darney's circuit, and we find him writing to Wesley in August in terms of warm brotherly affection. 'I confess', he declared, 'a perfect agreement between your sentiments, principles of religion, and my own'; his house and his pulpit, he wrote, would always be available for John and Charles on their travels.[62] In August 1748 Wesley was at Haworth, and preached to a congregation larger than the church could contain; even at five o'clock in the morning the church was packed to full capacity. The two friends then rode off over the moors for Roughlee in Lancashire, where they had to face a brutal assault by the Vicar of Colne at the head of his half-drunken rabble.[63] In 1751 Charles Wesley was at Haworth again, and wrote of his visit:

> I never saw the church better filled; but after I had preached in the pulpit the multitude in the churchyard cried out that they could not hear, and begged me to come forth. I did so, and preached on a tombstone. Between three and four thousand heard me gladly. At two, I called again to about double the number....The church leads and steeple were filled with people, all still as night. If ever I preached the gospel, I preached it then. The Lord take all the glory![64]

In May 1753 Grimshaw and Charles Wesley travelled together to Bolton and Manchester, and then to the Methodist Conference at Leeds;[65] then John Wesley rode with him to Haworth, and preached to 'a crowded congregation'.[66] In April 1755 Wesley rode for five hours through the rain to preach at Haworth at ten in the morning, and the throng of people from all quarters constrained him to preach again out of doors after midday.[67] In October 1756 Charles Wesley and Grimshaw preached and travelled side by side all through the northern circuit, taking Haworth *en route*. 'The church which hath been lately enlarged could scarce contain the congregation,' wrote Charles; 'we had a blessed number of communicants, and the Master of the Feast in the midst.'[68] They bade farewell to each other four days later, and Charles observed: 'I parted with my right hand, my brother and bosom-friend, Grimshaw.'[69] In 1757 John Wesley preached at Haworth again, and then travelled widely through the north with Grimshaw. On Sunday, May 22, he wrote:

After preaching at five, I took horse for Haworth. A December storm met us upon the mountain, but this did not hinder such a congregation as the church could not contain. I suppose we had near a thousand communicants, and scarce a trifler among them. In the afternoon, the church not containing more than a third of the people, I was constrained to be in the church-yard.[70]

In April 1759 Grimshaw met Wesley at Stainland, and they travelled on to Keighley.[71] Three months later Wesley was at Haworth again, and wrote of his visit:

Sunday, July 22nd; At ten, Mr Milner read prayers, but the church would not near contain the congregation; so after prayers I stood on a scaffold close to the church, and the congregation in the church-yard. The communicants alone filled the church. In the afternoon, the congregation was nearly doubled; and yet most of these were not curious hearers, but men fearing God.[72]

In April 1761 Wesley and Grimshaw were at Lower Darwen, near Blackburn,[73] and in July John was once more with his friend at Haworth; he was forced to mount a scaffold to reach the crowds who filled church and churchyard alike. 'The church would not near contain the people,' he wrote on July 12: 'what has God wrought in the midst of those rough mountains!'[74] And on July 16: 'I have been for some days with Mr Grimshaw, an Israelite indeed! A few such as he would make a nation tremble; he carries fire wherever he goes.'[75]

Grimshaw himself used to say that he had known the Wesleys first, and them he loved best; but he soon found in George Whitefield a friend who was second only to them. In 1748 Whitefield returned to England after four years in the New World, and in 1749 he journeyed through Yorkshire, preaching at Haworth and Ewood. There were some six thousand hearers in the churchyard, and about a thousand remained for a sacramental service of most awe-inspiring solemnity.[76] Once he climbed a scaffold to preach, and was observed to spend a few moments in prayer. Then he cast a long look over the hushed sea of faces, raised his hands, and implored the presence and blessing of God. Then he gave out his text with great solemnity: 'It is appointed unto men once to die, and after this, the judgment!' (Heb. 9: 27). There was a brief pause while silence settled still more firmly on the vast crowd; then a wild shriek burst from the midst of the congregation. Whitefield waited to learn the cause, keeping the crowd calm while Grimshaw made his way to the spot. A few moments later Grimshaw elbowed his way back and cried out to the preacher with the uncommon energy of concern and alarm: 'Brother Whitefield, you stand amongst the dead and the dying; an immortal soul has been called into eternity! The destroying angel is passing over the congregation; cry aloud, and spare not!' After the lapse of a moment or two he gave out the same text, and a thrill of awe spread over the vast crowd who heard him. Whitefield's life was full of drama, but he seldom spoke to a more intent and earnest multitude. Not a sound was heard as he went on in a strain of most tremendous eloquence to warn cold and Christless souls to flee from the wrath to come.[77]

In 1750 Whitefield met Ingham and Grimshaw at Leeds, and the crowds which came in from all quarters were far beyond all that they had ever before seen in Yorkshire. 'Last night', he wrote, 'I preached to many, many thousands, and this morning also at five o'clock. Methinks I am now got into another climate!'[78] He rode on to Haworth, whence he wrote to Hervey: 'The church was thrice filled with communicants; it was a precious season.'[79] In 1752 thousands flocked to wait on him at Haworth again[80] and in 1753 he had more numerous congregations both at Haworth and in Yorkshire than ever before.[81] Grimshaw said that in his church they dispensed the Lord's Supper 'to as many people as sipped away thirty-five bottles of wine within a gill; it was a high day indeed, a Sabbath of Sabbaths.'[82] In 1755 Grimshaw travelled with Whitefield as far afield as Stockport and Chinley, while at Haworth both the meadows and the woodlands above them were covered with crowds which had come from all parts. The Old Hundred, in the version by Watts, was sung at the close of a most solemn service; it was Grimshaw's favourite hymn, and the mighty volume of song from the thousands who sang echoed through the valley below with an effect which no words could describe.[83] In 1756 Whitefield preached at Haworth from a scaffold, and wrote of it in one of his letters: 'I have been in honest Mr Grimshaw's and Mr Ingham's round, preaching upon the mountains to many thousands....The Sacrament at Mr Grimshaw's was most awful.'[84] Samuel Whitaker was one member of that crowd who never forgot the day, and wrote of it long years after: 'I got among the crowd, nearly under the scaffold....Mr Whitefield spoke as if he had been privy to all my thoughts, words, and actions, from the tenth year of my age.'[85] Truly these were men of God, and days of the Son of Man!

Persecution was as real in Yorkshire as in other parts of England where the gospel was preached by men of the same stamp. The lay preachers sent out under Wesley and Ingham and Grimshaw had to put up with gross barbarities; mobs broke down the doors of private homes and plundered their goods. Some were held down under water till they were all but drowned; some were daubed all over with paint, and were pelted with egg-shells filled with blood and stopped with pitch.[86] Grimshaw himself met the roughest treatment in Colne, where the curate was most violently opposed to a society under Ingham. Grimshaw used to visit this class meeting, and the landlord of Colne told Joseph Williams, in 1747, that he had preached 'damnation beyond all sense and reason' in a two-hour sermon.[87] The Rev. George White, who was Curate of Colne, had been educated for the Roman Priesthood in France; but he had left the Church of Rome, and had been put in charge of both Colne and Marsden. He was shamefully neglectful of his duties, and was often absent from his parish for weeks on end; once he read the funeral rite twenty times in one night over the graves of those who had been buried while he was away. In August 1748 he preached and then published a long sermon against the Methodists, who were accused of 'a schismatical rebellion against the best of Churches...and a confusion not to be paralleled in any other Christian Dominion'.[88] His plan to save Colne from the Methodists was to muster a mob by beat of drum for the defence of Church and Realm. Ingham's journals still preserve a copy of one of the proclamations which he issued from the Market Cross: 'Notice is hereby given that if any man be mindful to enlist in his Majesty's Service under the command of the Rev. Mr George White, Commander-in-Chief... let him repair to the drum-head at the Cross where each man shall receive a pint of ale in advance, and all other proper encouragements.'[89] Within a month of this sermon Grimshaw and John Wesley rode to Roughlee, where they were joined by two laymen from the northern circuits. Wesley was in the midst of his sermon when they saw a drunken rabble, armed with clubs and staves and led on by a Deputy Constable, pouring downhill from Colne. The four preachers agreed to go with him to a Justice of the Peace some two miles away, at Barrowford, in order to avoid further trouble. They had the mob for an escort, and the journey was thick with blows and oaths. The magistrate at Barrowford tried to compel Wesley to pledge himself not to visit Roughlee again; but this, Wesley stoutly refused to do. He was detained for some two hours before he was allowed to leave, and then the mob pursued him with sticks and stones and curses; he was beaten to the ground, and driven back to the house. Grimshaw was attacked with desperate violence, and was covered with mire and sludge. Friends who had come with them were forced to run for life itself amid a storm of dirt and stones without regard to age or sex; some were beaten with clubs, and some trampled under foot in the mire. One man was forced to leap into the dark waters of a river; when he crawled out he was threatened again. Another was dragged by the hair of his head along the road, menaced with clubs and blows without mercy. The first of these died from shock and distress, and the other never fully recovered from his injuries.[90] Next day Wesley wrote to the magistrate, who like Gallio cared for none of these things:

'All this time you were talking of justice and law!...Proceed against us by Law, if you can or dare; but not by lawless violence, not by making a drunken, cursing, swearing, riotous mob both judge, jury, and executioner! This is flat rebellion, both against God and the King!'[91]

There was little that Grimshaw and Ingham could do in the teeth of mob law; but they were not to be cowed by local bullies, and they returned like Paul and Barnabas to the cities which had driven them out. One year later, in 1749, they went to a society meeting near Colne, in spite of the vicar and his rude larrikin partisans. They had scarcely begun with a hymn when the Rev. George White arrived with a Deputy Constable at the head of a mob. He stormed into the house, armed with a club, and the master of the house was threatened with the stocks and instant arrest. The meeting was broken up in a few moments, and the preachers were left face to face with the mob. White then tried to compel them to sign a bond that they would not preach at Colne for the space of a year, on pain of a fifty-pounds' fine. When they refused they were marched off by the Vicar's order to Colne itself, and the mob on the way did not spare to beat and abuse all who tried to befriend the two captive preachers. It was proposed more than once that the bond should be signed for a time limit of six months, or two months; at length they were offered freedom at once without a bond if they would pledge truth and honour not to preach in or near Colne again. But when it was clear that they would not fall in with any terms thus proposed they were dragged down the road, with clubs and sticks brandished over their heads to menace and annoy, with mud and dirt spattered over their clothes which were torn and dishevelled, until they reached the Swan Inn, where they were at length dismissed at White's pleasure. But they refused to be daunted by threats or fears for the future, for they rejoiced to be counted worthy to suffer such indignities for the sake of His Name.[92]

In the same year Grimshaw wrote and published a strong reply to White's sermon; there were six-and-eighty closely printed pages, and it was a vigorous defence of the Methodist preachers. Grimshaw was not the man to be mealy-mouthed in a war of this kind, and a clear sign of what White could expect was to be found in the psalm which figured on the title-page: 'Why boastest thou thyself in mischief, O mighty man? The goodness of God endureth continually. Thy tongue deviseth mischiefs; like a sharp razor, working deceitfully. Thou lovest evil more than good, and lying rather than to speak righteousness' (Ps. 52: 1-3). He went on to tell him that his sermon was 'full of palpable contradictions, absurdities, falsities, groundless suggestions, and malicious surmises, and in some sort, vindicates the people it was intended to asperse'.[93] White might strut on the stage at Colne as a local braggard, but he was no match for Grimshaw in a conflict like this; Grimshaw pressed down upon him like a giant, and with knotted club for a flail, he threshed him as a pompous priest and popish cheat. It was shameful enough that White had been gaoled for debts in Chester Castle; it was far worse that for three years he should have played the rake in London and elsewhere. And then, forsooth! all at once the cheat and rake became the virtuous and indignant champion of the Church! Was it any wonder that the doughty Grimshaw rolled out his wrath in no gentle accent, but dressed him down with a voice like thunder? But three years more and White was dead. 'He drank himself first into jail', Wesley records, 'and then into his grave.'[94] But he is said to have sent for Grimshaw on his death-bed, and to have begged the help of his prayers and instructions.[95]

These were hard years for Grimshaw in the way of preaching and travelling, and none but a man of iron constitution could have stood the wear and tear. He preached twice at Haworth on the Lord's Day, often riding across the moors early on the Sunday morning after a meeting at Ewood the night before;[96] and he never relaxed the twelve monthly meetings in his own home hamlets as well as the wider circuits in which sixty sermons or more were preached in the course of the month. Once he made an apology for not having paid a visit to a sick case on the ground that he had been called upon to preach more than thirty times in that week alone![97] Neither storm nor rain could keep him from his hearers; night and day were alike to him if he had to visit the sick. He knew what it was to preach to vast crowds, but he was no less the servant of the poor and the few. He would often trudge the lonely moors for miles in winter rain or bitter wind with cheerful heart to preach to some small group of the aged and needy;[98] he was even known to have walked not a few miles at night in storms of snow to bring help or comfort to the sick when few would venture out of their homes.[99] In January 1777 Fletcher of Madeley told one of his correspondents: 'You must not be above being employed in a little way; the great Mr Grimshaw was not above walking some miles to preach to seven or eight persons.'[100] On January 1, 1753 a man by the name of Burdsall was at a barn meeting in Bingley when Grimshaw arrived; he walked in, dressed as a layman, and well buttoned against the storm. He threw off his coat and gave out a hymn, which the people sang with a voice like the voice of many waters; then he joined in prayer, and took a Bible from his pocket, announced his text, and preached with power.[101] In all sorts of weather, out on moor or mountain, often drenched with rain, often chilled with frost, with no regular meals and sometimes nothing more than a crust, in cottage homes or farmers' barns, he never grew weary of his labours as an evangelist. Romaine said that friends would urge him to spare himself for his health's sake, but he would say: 'Let me labour now; I shall have rest enough by and by. I cannot do enough for Christ who has done so much for me.'[102]

And his success was as great as his labours. The tenor and energy of his preaching had been talked of since the early 'forties, and the church at Haworth had often been crowded by hundreds of strangers; the Lord had met them there with the blessings of grace, and the church was still as crowded when the rage for novelty was no more. These great congregations were a feature of his labours to the end of his life, and they would swell to yet larger numbers for the visits of George Whitefield and the Wesleys. There were hundreds at such times who knelt at the Lord's Table, feeling that those great occasions were in a peculiar sense days of the Son of Man. He once declared that of eighteen persons he had buried in the past year he had reason to think that sixteen of them had entered into the Kingdom of God.[103] In 1747 Joseph Williams said that he could reckon on at least 120 souls in his classes who were savingly renewed.[104] In 1760 he stood with John Newton on a hill near Haworth, and spoke of the early years when all was barren. He went on to say:

> Now, through the blessing of God, besides a considerable number whom I have seen or known to have departed this life like Simeon, rejoicing in the Lord's salvation, and besides five Dissenting Churches or congregations of which the ministers and nearly every one of the members were first awakened under my ministry, I have still at my Sacraments, according to the weather, from three hundred to five hundred communicants, of the far greater part of whom so far as man…may judge, I can give almost as particular an account as I can of myself.[105]

Newton says that if a stranger had stood on the same spot, whence he could see little save bare hills and bleak moors, he would scarcely think it were credible. 'But', he adds, 'I knew the man well, and of all the men I ever knew, I can think of no one who was less to be suspected of boasting than Mr Grimshaw.'[106] To this we need only add the voice of William Romaine: 'He preached Christ, and Christ alone, and God gave him very numerous seals to his ministry. Himself hath told me that not fewer than twelve hundred were in communion with him, most of whom in the judgment of charity, he could not but believe to be one with Christ.'[107]

Grimshaw was in fact as true an itinerant and as much a Methodist as the Wesleys, with but a single difference; he had a church and a parish, which they had not. In 1748 the circuit of Keighley or Haworth was one of the nine recognized

Methodist circuits; in 1753 it was linked, with that of Leeds, and was known as Yorkshire and Haworth.[108] Grimshaw was a regular visitor at class meetings in this circuit, while Wesley's lay preachers came to Haworth where they held their meetings in his kitchen. But he and Charles Wesley were most anxious that the Methodists should not leave the Church of England, and in 1755 he went to the conference at Leeds, determined to take his leave of them if they should take theirs of the Church.[109] In 1758 he built a small chapel within his own parish in the fear that his flock might yet be turned over to a hireling shepherd; it was never used in his own lifetime, and he went on entertaining the lay preachers in his hospitable kitchen. But in 1760 some lay preachers applied for a licence as Dissenters, and he wrote to Charles Wesley to say that he would be forced to 'disown all connection with the Methodists'.[110] Charles read out this letter to the leaders with most salutary effects; 'all cried out against the licensed preachers.'[111] Grimshaw broke through the rules of Church Order at many points, and his labours led to a new burst of vigour in the Nonconformist circles; but he was at heart a staunch son of the Church of England, and he was grieved when his converts threw in their lot with these outside bodies. 'I believe', wrote Newton, 'that the number of those who remained in communion with him to the end of life was much greater than those who withdrew from him. With regard to the latter, the most that can be said against him, if it be indeed against him, is that he found them little better than heathen, and left them Evangelical Dissenters.'[112] And John Wesley never lost his warmth of feeling for his old friend Grimshaw; on April 14, 1779 we find in his *Journal* one brief but most ample remark: 'I lodged at the Ewood, which I still love for good Mr Grimshaw's sake.'[113]

Grimshaw had a mind too noble and a heart too benevolent to be fettered by an undue regard for mere names or parties, and he always preserved a close friendship with both Whitefield and the Wesleys. They in turn put him in touch with other men of like mind and heart in the gospel, and he came to know all the chief men in the great spiritual movement of that epoch. It was through George Whitefield and Lady Huntingdon that the friendship grew up between him and William Romaine, and the latter broke through his own rules to preach for Grimshaw in the open air at Haworth.[114] In 1760, and again in 1762, we are told of Romaine's visits to Haworth, and his testimony to Grimshaw is still in our hearing: 'He was the most humble walker with God I ever met with.'[115] In June 1757 John Newton took his first journey into Yorkshire, and was Grimshaw's guest at Haworth. 'Had it been the will of God', he wrote, 'methought I could have renounced the world to have lived in these mountains with such a minister!'[116] In August 1760 Newton spent a Sabbath with him, and preached as a layman to 150 people in his house.[117] Newton found in Grimshaw one whom he ranked next to Whitefield in his veneration and love, and in 1761 he was his guest again. He wrote:

> I number it amongst the many great mercies of my life, that I was favoured with his notice, edified by his instruction and example, and encouraged and directed by his advice, at the critical time when my own mind was much engaged with a desire of entering the ministry. I saw in him much more clearly than I could have learned from books or lectures what it was to be a faithful and exemplary minister of the gospel.'[118]

Then in 1759 Henry Venn was moved from Clapham to Huddersfield, where he became a near neighbour to Grimshaw at Haworth, and his own ministry of fire and devotion owed not a little to the ripe friendship that bound them heart to heart. Venn saw that he was an eminent instrument in the hand of God for winning the souls of men, and he believed that few men had ever shown such ardour in the service of Christ.[119] In June 1779 he wrote to his own son: 'There is nothing that I know of worthy a thought compared with possessing so much grace that everyone who comes near you is enlivened and edified in his own soul. Thus it was with my very dear friend, now high in glory, Mr Grimshaw.'[120]

Grimshaw was both thick and broad-set, short of stature, sharp in feature, strong in frame and robust in health; only once in twenty-one years was he stayed from duty by an illness while at Haworth.[121] Grimshaw was twice married, and twice mourned the death of a wife. In 1749 he made one of his few journeys away from the north, and preached in Bristol; he was no doubt on a visit to his daughter who had gone to Wesley's school at Kingswood. But in 1750 she ailed and passed away at the age of twelve; Charles Wesley said that she 'departed in the Lord'.[122] His son survived him by three years, and died childless; he was careless in his father's lifetime, but there was hope on his death-bed. Grimshaw was a man of rare charity, rich in brotherly affection; he loved all who loved Christ, and cared not what name or party they owned.[123] 'Indeed, Mr Grimshaw was one of God's servants,' wrote Venn, 'and of so loving a disposition, I scarce ever saw anyone go beyond him, and very few of the dearest of God's sons and daughters are so affectionate.'[124] Love for souls was the great master motive of his ministry, and this explains all that was eccentric or out of the common in his life and preaching. If he were quaint in speech or unorthodox in approach, he was always in earnest and always devout. His dress was plain, and may have been shabby at times; often he had but a single coat, and one pair of shoes. His food, like his clothing, was plain in the extreme, and he hated waste in all forms.[125] When his own house was full of guests he would sleep out in a hayloft, and rise betimes to clean their boots with his own hands.[126] One great secret of his life lay in the fact that he was a man of prayer; and his prayers in public had their root in the prayer life of his own home. In 1734 he began the custom of prayer four times a day, and we never hear that he broke it off. In his one-and-twenty years at Haworth he held household worship at five o'clock each day in the summer and six o'clock in the winter. He would retire at night after prayers with his family at eleven o'clock, and he loved to ejaculate throughout the day in terms of prayer: 'My God, my Jesus, I love Thee indeed; but how shall I love Thee enough?'[127]

Grimshaw's *Answer to White* was his only formal publication, but there are one or two other papers which have come down to us. Thus in 1744 he drew up a personal Covenant with God, and it was his custom in later life to renew it each quarter with fasting. In 1754 a short form of covenant was penned on the fly-leaf of his Bible, and these two documents are a striking witness to his piety and his convictions. In December 1762, four months before his death, he sent Romaine a clear statement as to his Creed; he was a Calvinist on his knees and an Arminian on his feet, and he tried to strike a proper balance between the two. He held that the doctrine of God's Elect was of special value for the assured, but he could not believe that it was a useful doctrine for the unconverted. 'My business', he said, 'is to invite all to come to Christ for salvation, and to assure all that will come of a hearty welcome.'[128] Newton thought him on the whole a Calvinist, but was not sure that he would have reckoned himself in that category. 'And many Calvinists', he went on to add, 'would scarcely have acknowledged his claim to that name if he had made it.'[129] His scant literary remains are a graphic witness to his mode of self-expression as well as to the great topics on which he loved to dwell. They still furnish us with a good idea of what his form as a preacher must have been like, for he clearly wrote in the same tenor as that in which he thought and spoke. Thus there is his testimony to the faithfulness of God: 'Why, before the Lord will suffer His promises to fail, He will lay aside His Divinity, He will un-God Himself!'[130] His Creed and Covenants are the overflowings of a heart full of Christ and the Scriptures, full of deep thoughts on the vileness of sin and the value of souls, the need for repentance, the call to holiness, and the life of the world to come.[131] 'When I die', he said, 'I shall then have my greatest grief and my greatest joy; my greatest grief that I have done so little for Jesus, and my greatest joy that Jesus has done so much for me.'[132]

Grimshaw had led a most active life all along, and his last year was as busy as all his days had been; none of his great evangelical contemporaries had worked harder than he, and few had worked so hard. In August 1762 Lady Huntingdon was in Yorkshire with Whitefield and Romaine as her chaplains, and days as the days of the Son of Man dawned at Haworth once more. Three months later, in November 1762, Grimshaw poured out his hopes in a letter to the Countess:

> I hope ere long to see my dear brother Whitefield in his own pulpit again. When will Your Ladyship revive us with another visit? What blessings did the Lord shower upon us the last time you were here! And how did our hearts burn within us to proclaim His love and grace to perishing sinners! Come and animate us afresh; aid us by your counsels and your prayers; communicate a spark of your glowing zeal, and stir us up to renewed activity in the cause of God![133]

Early in March 1763 Whitefield passed through Yorkshire and preached in old centres on his way to Scotland, where he embarked for the New World; but it would seem that he did not call at Haworth, where a 'putrid fever' had broken out and was dark with omens of worse to come.[134] Had he known that Grimshaw was to fall a victim before the scourge, would be in fact on his death-bed, we cannot but believe that he would have risked all, as did Venn and Ingham, to be at his friend's side. Grimshaw knew that this plague was highly infectious, and felt that his house could not be immune; but he would not desist from the call to visit the sick and the dying. Soon he caught it, and knew that he would die; but though he had to look into the cold, clear eyes of Death, his look was that 'of one to whom it seemed as though it were the face of an angel.' April saw Newton in Yorkshire again, and May found John Wesley on his way there; but that 'great Apostle of the North, the revered Mr Grimshaw,' was then no more.[135]

The news of his illness found its way out over the hills to Ingham at Aberford and Venn at Huddersfield as the month of March wore slowly away. Ingham twice rode over from Aberford to see him, and later told Lady Huntingdon what had transpired. Grimshaw greeted him on his first visit with the remark: 'My last enemy is come! The signs of death are upon me. But I am not afraid—No! No! Blessed be God, my hope is sure, and I am in His hands.' Ingham found him much worse on his second visit, and he knelt by his side in prayer. Grimshaw said: 'I harbour no desire of life; my time is come, and I am wholly resigned to God.' Then he raised eyes and hands towards heaven, and said: 'Tell her Ladyship…that I thank her from the bottom of my heart for all her kindnesses to me during the years that I have known her. With my dying breath, I implore every blessing, temporal and spiritual, to rest upon her!' Later, he placed his hand over his heart, and said: 'I am quite exhausted, but I shall soon be at home for ever with the Lord, a poor miserable sinner redeemed by His blood.'[136] Henry Venn came in as Ingham bade his old friend the last farewell, and asked him how he felt. 'As happy as I can be on earth', was the reply, 'and as sure of glory as if I was in it.' He was conscious of the love and presence of God in a way such as he had not been since the days of his first joy: 'Never', he said, 'have I had such a visit from God since I knew Him.' The end drew near, and he was in a state of high fever; but one of the servants asked how he was, and he replied: 'I have nothing to do but to step out of my bed into heaven; I have my foot on its threshold already.'[137] On April 7 Venn wrote: 'He lies ill of a very dangerous fever, and how the great Lord of the Harvest designs to dispose of him, I know not. But whenever he enters into rest, one of the great ornaments of the gospel will be taken from us.'[138] That very day, at the age of fifty-four, his spirit fled with the last soft and lovely murmur 'Here goes an unprofitable servant!'[139] It was Henry Venn who gave the funeral oration both at Luddenden where he was buried and at Haworth where his years had been spent; and his voice rose on the air like the full tones of a bell as he gave out the text so dear to the heart of his friend: 'For to me to live is Christ, and to die is gain' (Phil. 1: 21).

Bibliography

John Newton, *Memoirs of the Life of the late Rev. William Grimshaw, A.B., with occasional reflections; in Six Letters to the Rev. Henry Foster* (1799).

George G. Cragg, *Grimshaw of Haworth* (The Canterbury Press, 1948).

John Charles Ryle, 'William Grimshaw and His Ministry', *Chapter V in Christian Leaders of the Last Century* (New Ed., 1880).

'A Member of the Houses of Shirley and Hastings', *The Life and Times of Selina, Countess of Huntingdon* (1839).

Thomas Jackson, *The Journal of the Rev. Charles Wesley, M.A.* (First Ed., 1849).

Nehemiah Curnock, *The Journal of the Rev. John Wesley, A.M.* (Bicentenary Issue, 1938).

John Telford, *The Letters of the Rev John Wesley, A.M.* (Standard Ed., 1931).

Luke Tyerman, *The Life and Times of the Rev. John Wesley* (4th Ed., 1878).

Luke Tyerman, *The Life of the Rev. George Whitefield* (2nd Ed., 1890).

Luke Tyerman, 'The Rev. Benjamin Ingham', Chapter iii in *The Oxford Methodists* (1878).

Josiah Bull, *John Newton* (2nd Ed., 1868).

Mrs. Gaskell, *The Life of Charlotte Brontë* (1900).

James Stephen, *Essays in Ecclesiastical Biography* (New Ed., 1875).

G. R. Balleine, *A History of the Evangelical Party* (New Ed., 1933).

HERE LIE
THE EARTHLY REMAINS OF
JOHN BERRIDGE
LATE VICAR OF EVERTON
AND AN ITINERANT SERVANT OF JESUS CHRIST
WHO LOVED HIS MASTER AND HIS WORK
AND AFTER RUNNING ON HIS ERRANDS MANY YEARS WAS
CALLED UP TO WAIT ON HIM ABOVE.

READER,
ART THOU BORN AGAIN?
NO SALVATION WITHOUT A NEW BIRTH!
I WAS BORN IN SIN FEBRUARY 1716
REMAINED IGNORANT OF MY FALLEN STATE TILL 1730
LIVED PROUDLY ON FAITH AND WORKS FOR SALVATION TILL
1754
ADMITTED TO EVERTON VICARAGE 1755
FLED TO JESUS ALONE FOR REFUGE 1756
FELL ASLEEP IN CHRIST JANUARY 22ND 1793.

His own Epitaph, except the date of his death
(Works, p. 66)

2

John Berridge
1716–93

John Berridge was born at Kingston in Nottinghamshire on March 1, 1716, the first of four sons in the home of a wealthy farmer. But though he was country born, he was virtually city bred, for he spent the greater part of his first fourteen years with an aunt who lived in Nottingham. There the groundwork of his education was laid, but there was no special sign of promise for the future. He was remarkable in his boyhood for piety and steadiness, but he had no real grasp of the gospel. He was induced to read and pray with a lad of his own age who set out to win his soul for Christ, and he in turn began to read and pray with some of his schoolmates. At the age of fourteen he had become convinced that he was a sinner, but he knew not the way of the new birth. It was just then that he left school and lost his friends, for his father thought that the time had come for him to learn 'the ins and outs' of a farmer's career. It did not seem too late to make him a son of the soil, and his father hoped to train him as the heir of his own holdings; thus he took the lad off to the local fairs, and tried to teach him how to think in terms of fat stock and their market value. But he was so consistently at fault in his judgment that he drove his father at length into complete despair of him as a recruit for agriculture. No doubt there was a hard struggle before the old farmer gave way, but his distaste for a farmer's calling and his utter failure to judge the price of fat stock were deep and immovable. And all this while, so strong was his bias in the way of prayer and reading that his family grew more and more anxious as to what it should mean. But it was his father who cast the die with the ready insight of a man who was wont to read the signs of nature. 'John,' he said, 'I find you are unable to form any practical idea of the price of cattle, and therefore I shall send you to college to be a light to the Gentiles!'[1]

Thus on October 28, 1734, at the age of eighteen, he was entered at Clare Hall in Cambridge, and he at once settled down to apply himself with uncommon avidity to his studies. He took the degree of B.A. in 1738 and of M.A. in 1742, but his thirst for knowledge could not even be quenched by his accession to a Fellowship. It was said that all through the years from 1734 to 1756 he gave fifteen hours a day to study, and he read so hard in those years that he mastered the whole world of literature. Henry Venn who knew him for fifty years said that he was as familiar with Greek and Latin as he was with his own mother tongue.[2] He won a high reputation as a thorough scholar, and once at least he was Moderator in the Schools for Cambridge.[3] This wide learning gave him a place that was second to none among his own colleagues, but he also possessed a turn of mind for wit which made him a popular companion in all circles. This strong vein of humour was fed on the quips of Hudibras which he could quote with such aptitude that he became increasingly well known as a clever, learned, and witty don. If it were known that he would be present at a public dinner, it meant that his table would be crowded with guests who were captivated by his wit and conversation. People of high rank sought him out, and men like the elder Pitt's nephew were among his more intimate companions. There was a strain of the odd and eccentric in his character from the beginning, and that strain found freedom for its full play in those carefree days at Clare Hall. It was perhaps his wit rather than his learning that most endeared him to others; his gaiety and oddity alike made him the best companion in the world. But though the name of John Berridge was much spoken against in his after career, no one ever thought to deny his great merit and real ability as a student of the Classics.

Berridge must have taken Orders in the 'forties as a Fellow of Clare, but his early zeal for the things of God had long since grown cold and indifferent. He knew little of the plague of his heart, and less of Christ as the Saviour. He drank deeply from the poison cup of Socinian scepticism, and for ten years, except for a few brief intervals, he gave up his early habits of prayer. In these intervals he would weep with bitter regret at the sad state into which he had sunk compared with the frame of mind in which he had first come to Clare Hall. We can still catch the throb of deep remorse: 'O that it were with me as in years past!'[4] Ryle's frank comment was: how hardly shall they that are Fellows of a College in Oxford or Cambridge enter the Kingdom of God![5] It was of God's mercy alone that he did not sink beneath the waters, never to rise again. Smyth points out that, on the human side, he was saved by the fact that he had such an 'acute intelligence of the academic pattern', for it helped him to see that there was an almost insensible drift from Socinian doubt into rank atheism.[6] He soon perceived that views which made less of God the Son would in the end make less of God the Father, while the kind of morality which they fostered was no higher in its claims and standards than that which the world at large would gladly approve. Thus his very scepticism made him sceptical of his unbelief, and he fought his way back to the orthodox position of truth. With the recovery of his faith he resumed the regular exercise of his devotions, and in 1749, after years of idleness, he accepted the curacy of Stapleford. This he served for six years from his college, and he took great trouble with his ignorant and dissolute flock. He pressed upon them the necessity of sanctification, but, to his own grief and disappointment, there was not the slightest change in their lives. It was well that he should seek the good of their souls, but his own soul was still in need of light.

On July 7, 1755 he was appointed to the Bedfordshire cure of Everton, a small living in the gift of Clare Hall, and he lived in the vicarage from that day on till the day of his death. Here he at once began to preach in the same strain as in his last parish, but not one soul was brought to Christ. He was already popular as a preacher and much followed by his country hearers, for his sermons were plain, striking, and most impressive in style and delivery; but he aimed at reformation of the outward life by a mixed doctrine of faith and works, and he found that he could do no more than knock off their fine caps and bonnets.[7] His own life was strictly moral and correct, and his diligence as a pastor was never in question; but his efforts were all fruitless, and his people were as unsanctified as they ever had been. His own views of salvation were much like 'a solar system without the sun', and the result was that he could transmit no light to his congregation.[8] He thought himself on the right path to heaven while he was as yet wholly out of the way, and he believed that he was a pilgrim for the City of God when he had not even begun to look thither.[9] He kept up this style of preaching for a year and a half, but his second Christmas found him burdened with a sense of discouragement. The doubt at last sprang up in his mind that perhaps he was not right himself, and this insistent misgiving grew so strong that he found it too painful to bear. It drove him to his knees, and he began to call upon the Lord night and day with intense desire: 'Lord, if I am right, keep me so; if I am not right, make me so. Lead me to the knowledge of the truth as it is in Jesus.'[10] He had no friend to whom he could go for advice, but this was a cry that the Lord Himself was bound to hear. He was not right, but grace would make him so.

He was kept in travail of soul for some ten days, but then it pleased the Lord abundantly to grant his prayer. He was sitting quietly in his house one morning, musing on a text of Scripture, when there flashed through his mind certain words with wonderful vividness: 'Cease from thine own works' (see Prov. 23: 4; Heb. 4: 10) His mind had been in a frame of deep calm, but this broke in on him like a voice from heaven. He found himself plunged into a tempest of strong feeling, and a torrent of tears rained down his cheeks. The veil was torn from his eyes, and he saw how he had been stumbled by the same rock ever since he had been a lad fourteen years old; and that rock was just some secret trust in his own works as the ground of his hope for glory. 'I had hoped to be saved partly in my own name and partly in Christ's Name,' he wrote on July 3, 1758 'though I am told there is salvation in no other name except in the Name of Jesus Christ.'[11] His first collected reaction was to begin thinking about the words 'faith' and 'believe'; he turned to his Concordance, and was amazed to find that they ran through many columns.[12] It was from that moment that he formed the resolution to preach only Jesus Christ and His Salvation by faith, and the whole tone of his ministry was to be changed by that decision. At the age of forty-two, in the prime of health and intellect, he was suddenly transformed from a prophet of good morals into a preacher of the gospel. He was well read, far from a fool, a man of recognized scholarship and classical distinction; and yet he was radically changed in his own innermost heart by the power of the Evangel. He had no earthly friend for guide, yet he had come to hold the same gospel as men like Whitefield held. This was surely nothing less than the touch of the finger of God!

He drew up two or three sermons on this basis as an experiment, and it made his preaching more pointed than ever. Some of his old hearers were vexed or surprised by his new doctrine, but most of the congregation soon felt the power of a deep and tremendous conviction. After he had tried out this new message for two or three Sundays, he was still in some doubt lest he were not yet right as he could not perceive any better effects than from his old sermons. But one of his parishioners at this crucial moment came to ask his counsel. 'Well, Sarah,' he began, as a kind of greeting; but she replied: 'Well, not so well I fear.' He was surprised, and asked: 'Why, what is the matter, Sarah?' And back came the reply: 'Matter! Why, I don't know what's the matter. These new sermons! I find we are all to be lost now, I can neither eat, drink, nor sleep. I don't know what's to become of me!'[13] The same week brought two or three more on like errands, and he was so confirmed by their visits in his belief that his recent change of heart was from God that he resolved henceforth to know and preach nothing but Christ and Him crucified. He burnt his old sermons forthwith, and soon dropped all written sermons as well; the church was soon crowded, and God began to seal his new testimony with the conviction and conversion of many of his hearers. 'I preached up sanctification by the works of the Law very earnestly for six years in a former parish, and never brought one soul to Christ,' he wrote. 'I did the same in this parish for two years without any success at all. But as soon as ever I preached Jesus Christ and faith in His blood, then believers were added to the church continually; then people flocked from all parts to hear the glorious sound of the gospel, some coming six miles, others eight, and others ten, and that constantly.'[14]

His new style of preaching was soon the talk of the country, for it frightened as well as fascinated his auditory; he told them so plainly that they were the children of wrath, and that none but Christ could save them![15] Within three months seven people in his parish had been thoroughly converted, and there were nine or ten more from Potton, two from Eaton, and two from Gamlingay for whom he was very hopeful.[16] News of all this came to Wesley's ears in April 1758 through a letter in which Berridge gave an account of his converts; but such a storm was in the air that he knew not how it would end! It had begun to whistle about his ears when twelve local clergy combined in opposition to him, and when the Squire warned his tenants that they were not to hear him on pain of eviction.[17] On June 2,

John Walsh rode over from Bedford to see how the land lay, and he told John Wesley: 'He meets little companies of his converts from several towns and villages at his own house....The country seems to kindle round him.'[18] On June 22 he moved outside his own parish bounds and began to preach in barns and farmhouses to all who would hear the gospel.[19] In July George Whitefield passed through on his way to Scotland, and gladly preached at his request. 'Mr Berridge,' he wrote on July 31, 1758, 'who was lately awakened at Everton, promises to be a burning and shining light.'[20] On August 1 God was pleased to bless his itinerant preaching to a neighbour, William Hicks, the Vicar of Wrestlingworth, some four miles from Everton. Hicks had been so hostile at first that he even refused the Lord's Supper to those of his parishioners who went to hear Berridge; now he joined hands with him in a lifelong partnership of service and soul-winning.[21] On November 6 Wesley himself arrived at Everton, and his journal records the fact that he preached at six in the evening and at five in the morning before he rode on to the London Foundery.[22]

The year 1759 was for ever memorable in the Everton Revival. On March 3 Wesley arrived at four o'clock. 'Mr Berridge did not expect me till the next day,' he wrote, 'so he thought it best I should preach in his house.'[23] The next evening he preached to a full church and then rode on to Colchester. But on March 10 he wrote to Lady Huntingdon:

> Mr Berridge appears to be one of the most simple as well as one of the most sensible men of all whom it has pleased God to employ in reviving primitive Christianity...They come near twelve or fourteen miles to hear him, and very few come in vain. His word is with power; he speaks as plain and home as John Nelson, but with all the propriety of Mr Romaine and tenderness of Mr Hervey.[24]

On May 14 he preached for the first time outside church or cottage; it is described in one of his letters:

On Monday se'nnight, Mr Hicks accompanied me to Meldred. On the way, we called at a farmer's house. After dinner I went into his yard, and seeing near one hundred and fifty people, I called for a table and preached for the first time in the open air. Two persons were seized with strong convictions, fell down, and cried out most bitterly. We then went to Meldred, where I preached in a field to about four thousand people. In the morning at five, Mr Hicks preached in the same field to about a thousand. And now the presence of the Lord was wonderfully among us. There was abundance of weeping and strong crying, and I trust, beside many that were slightly wounded, near thirty received true heart-felt conviction.'[25]

Hicks and Berridge then set out for home, but called at the farm on their way and began to speak to a dozen or so in the brew-house with most astonishing effect. He preached again in his own house at four in the afternoon, and the Spirit of God brought the consolation of the gospel to yet one more who was in need. But the phenomena of strong religious emotion now broke out, and spiritual hysteria spread like wildfire.

On Sunday May 20 there were amazing scenes; an eye-witness described them to Wesley in a letter which he transcribed for his *Journal*. At the morning service many fainted or cried out in alarm while Berridge was preaching. 'The Church was equally crowded in the afternoon,' so runs the account, 'the windows being filled within and without, and even the outside of the pulpit to the very top, so that Mr Berridge seemed almost stifled by their very breath.'[26] There were perhaps three times as many men as there were women present; thirty of them had left their homes at two in the morning to walk from a village thirteen miles away.

The presence of God really filled the place. And while poor sinners felt the presence of death in their souls, what sounds of distress did I hear! The greatest number of them who cried or fell were men; but some women and several children felt the power of the same almighty Spirit and seemed just sinking into hell...And indeed almost all the cries were like those of human creatures dying in bitter anguish. Great numbers wept without any noise; others fell down as dead; some sinking in silence, some with extreme noise and violent agitation.'[27]

This eye-witness stood on one of the pews to keep track of it all and was thrilled with momentary dread as one here and one there dropped; for one may feel the blast, though it is his neighbour who is killed by the cannonball. Those who knew the Lord were heard to laugh with gladness, 'till the cries of them who were struck with the arrows of conviction were almost lost in the sounds of joy'. [28] When the service came to an end they all crowded into the vicarage where the work still went on.

And now I did see such a sight as I do not expect again on this side eternity. The faces of...all the believers present did really shine; and such a beauty, such a look of extreme happiness and at the same time of divine love and simplicity did I never see in human faces till now.[29]

The crowds which thronged to hear him from all parts of the country were thus moved to cry out with tears and groans under the power of his preaching and the awe of divine glory. Some fell into a kind of trance or some form of catalepsy; others were thrown into bitter cries and frightening convulsions. The same remarkable phenomena had marked Wesley's preaching in London and Bristol just twenty years before, but were almost unknown in George Whitefield's experience and were greatly disliked by Charles Wesley. All that Wesley saw in 1739 was to be seen again by men such as Burns and M'Cheyne at Dundee in 1839. It was as though eternity were made so real that the feelings of the people could not be held in leash. There would be the hush of breathless silence as each hearer was caught in rapt attention; then half-suppressed sighs would break from many a heart, and tears would bathe the face. Some would cry as if they had been pierced with a dart; some could neither walk nor stand by themselves.[30] And such were the mysterious phenomena which

came to light under the preaching of Berridge all through that
first summer, though he never played on the taut feelings of his
hearers for the purpose nor set any great store by such signs
when they did appear. Sometimes men would struggle in such
anguish of mind that the very pews were broken; sometimes
they would sit through all that they heard as if unaffected, and
then would drop on their way home. They would fall down like
dead men and lie where they fell, on the road or in his garden, for
they could not even walk the short two hundred yard path from
the church to his house. Both Wesley and Berridge watched it
all at the time with a sense of awe and caution, but we need
not now feel concerned either to defend or explain these things;
they passed away in course of time, but they were a sign to many
that God was there in power both to wound and to heal.

This work of grace was soon to spread through the neighbour
counties, but it flourished nowhere more than in the east and
north of Bedford. On Monday evening, May 21, Berridge
preached on Shelford Common, twenty miles away from Everton
and four from Cambridge. He was feeling sick with fatigue, but
still strong in spirit. He wrote:

> A table was set for me on the Common, and to my great
> surprise, I found near ten thousand people round it, among
> whom were many gownsmen from Cambridge. I was hardly
> able to stand on my feet, and extremely hoarse with a cold.
> When I lifted up my foot to get on the table a horrible dread
> overwhelmed me; but the moment I was fixed there-on,
> I seemed as unconcerned as a statue.'[31]

He preached again in the morning to a thousand or so, and
then agreed with Hicks to go into Hertford. They would travel
with each other at first, and then would separate so that larger
numbers might hear the Word of Life; they would preach in the
fields or in any other place that offered, and would devote four
days each week to this itinerant labour. This was the first plan
for the work which from that time forth with little interruption
throughout the next twenty-four years was to fill his life in

preaching the good news from heaven.[32] Except for a yearly visit to London, he seldom went far beyond his own district; but that district embraced every part of the counties of Bedford, Cambridge, Hertford, Essex, Suffolk and Huntingdon. He chose as his watchword the great ordination charge to seek for Christ's sheep that are dispersed abroad, and he often rode a hundred miles to preach a dozen sermons in the course of a week.[33] In the first twelve months of his work with Hicks no less than four thousand people were roused to a concern for their souls; that alone may give some small idea of how much good was wrought in his career as an itinerant preacher which now began.[34]

Meanwhile, Lady Huntingdon asked Romaine and Madan as her chaplains to visit Everton, and they were warmly received by Hicks and Berridge. They were amazed at what they saw, and felt some doubt at first as to whether it was of God; but the artless testimony of some of the children and a preaching tour with Berridge cleared up their minds. The facts of this tour are detailed in an account sent by John Walsh to John Wesley, and now preserved in his *Journal*. On July 14 Berridge preached to the crowds in the churchyard, and one man was so struck that his 'shaking exceeded that of a cloth in the wind; it seemed as if the Lord came upon him like a giant, taking him by the neck and shaking all his bones in pieces'.[35] He was greatly fatigued, but he went on preaching daily to thousands. On July 18 he reached Stapleford where he had been curate for some six years, and his heart was more than usually drawn out to those who had never heard the gospel from his lips till that night. There were about fifteen hundred who met in a close to hear him, and the power of God was so marked that he was kept up till a late hour to comfort troubled men and women.[36] On July 19 some two thousand people gathered in a close at Triplow, and the cries of those who were in anguish of soul gave great offence to a few who sat on horseback on the fringe of the crowd. Berridge could not dismiss the crowds; an hour later most of them were still in the house or the orchard where sighs and tears mingled with praise and prayers.[37] On July 20 he preached again at Everton;

'I shook from head to foot', wrote one of his helpers, 'while tears of joy ran down my face.'[38] Then, on Sunday July 22, the church was packed, and hundreds stood without. 'And now the arrows of God flew abroad!...We found about two hundred persons, chiefly men, who cried aloud for mercy; but many more were affected, perhaps as deeply, though in a calmer way.'[39] In great weakness, he preached again after lunch in the close; but God strengthened him, and poured out a fresh flood of blessing.

Romaine and Madan returned to London full of astonishment at all that God had wrought, but the flow of visitors to the scene of Revival was still maintained. On August 5 John Wesley paid his second visit to the Everton Vicarage, though he only stayed for one night. He was interested to find that the more violent phenomena had begun to abate, a fact which he thought to be in keeping with the course of events in London and Bristol twenty years before.[40] On August 28 he was back for a night, and preached again to a crowded congregation; there were convulsions, and some conversions![41] In the month of November Berridge was summoned to preach before the University of Cambridge, and this meant an absence of four Sundays from his own church. Wesley arranged to take his place for one week-end, and arrived in Everton on the Saturday. Many came to the house in the evening, and it was a time of great joy. Then, on Sunday November 25, he preached in the morning and afternoon, and the Lord was remarkably present with him. But he observed a great change in the way that things went on. No one fell down, or was convulsed; no one cried out, or lapsed into a trance. 'Only some trembled exceedingly, a low murmur was heard, and many were refreshed with the multitude of peace.'[42] But there were four Sundays in all for which Berridge had need of help, and Lady Huntingdon arranged with John Fletcher to pay him a visit. He made himself known to Berridge simply as a recent convert who would be glad of his help and counsel. His name was not mentioned at all, but his slightly foreign accent gave him away. Berridge learned that he was a Swiss from the canton of Berne, and asked for news of John Fletcher. Then his identity could no longer be hid, and the vicar gladly asked him to preach for him on the morrow. It was the first memorable meeting between two remarkable men![43]

No doubt Fletcher informed Lady Huntingdon of all that he now saw, and the Countess resolved to join him, with Venn and Madan, at Everton. She and her friends could stay only for three short days, but their visit caused a great stir; vast crowds streamed in to the little village, and nine sermons were preached during their stay. At seven o'clock the morning after they all arrived, Berridge preached to a huge crowd in a field close to the church, and the power of God fell upon them with uncommon majesty. At eleven o'clock Hicks read prayers in the church, and Venn preached on the joy that is felt in heaven for one sinner that repenteth. That afternoon the church could not contain one-fifth of the amazing multitude, so that Martin Madan stood and cried in the open air: 'If any man thirst, let him come unto Me and drink' (John 7: 37). On the second morning Fletcher read the prayers while Madan preached on the need for the new birth to a congregation that packed the church to excess. Berridge read prayers in the afternoon while Venn was the preacher; but so many were still outside the church that the vicar himself went out when the service had come to an end and preached to them in the open air. On the third day it was judged that the crowds had grown to ten thousand, and Venn began the day's preaching from that great text: 'The harvest is past, the summer is ended, and we are not saved' (Jer. 8: 20). The whole crowd was deeply moved, and many sank down and wept grievously. There were even larger numbers at the afternoon service, and picturesque indeed must have been the sight as they flocked to that Hill of Zion. The last sermon was given by Berridge, whose voice floated out on the calm evening air to bid them behold the Lamb of God. There was astonishing power in that call, but he closed in silence and the crowds went away with the words of one of Wesley's noblest hymns still thrilling heart and mind with solemn grandeur.[44] This was in some sense the end of that remarkable year in the Everton Revival, for while Madan was left in charge, the good Countess carried Berridge back to London to meet her friends and to preach for Whitefield in his City Tabernacle. But his course was now fixed as an itinerant preacher in the Everton countryside, and no vicar in the south of England ever defied Church Order so freely as did Berridge. 'And sure there is a cause', he wrote to John Thornton on August 10, 1774, 'when souls are perishing for lack of knowledge.'[45] That was his great defence; he had no time to make scruples on Church Order when the one need was to preach the gospel to the dying. In an undated letter to an unnamed clergyman he wrote:

> If every parish were blessed with a gospel minister, there could be little need of itinerant preaching; but since these ministers are thinly scattered about the country and neighbouring pulpits are usually locked up against them, it behoves them to take advantage of fields or barns to cast abroad the gospel seed.'[46]

He called himself a Riding Pedlar who was compelled to serve some forty centres besides his own parish,[47] or a Rambling Bishop who was obliged to spread the gospel message beyond his own borders.[48] Mobility and stamina were thus prerequisites for the discharge of the duties of a preacher as he saw them; yet his own possession of these two qualities in high degree was no proof in itself that this concept was right.[49] He could warmly approve the Liturgy and Articles of the Church of England, and bless God for a church in which to preach; but the general character of laymen and clergy made him fear lest God should withdraw His grace from both Church and nation.[50] Thus he cared but little for Church Order if he could only reach men's souls, and his itinerant labours in the parishes of his brother clergy were the means of planting Nonconformist congregations in at least a dozen county towns or hamlets.[51]

Canon Smyth holds that this impatience with Church Order was in the last analysis due to deep-seated misgivings about the Church of England.[52] Thus in 1777 he wrote to Lady Huntingdon:

What has become of Mr Venn's Yorkshire flock? What will become of his Yelling flock, or of my flocks, at our decease? Or what will become of your students at your removal? They are virtual Dissenters now, and will be Dissenters then. And the same will happen to many, perhaps most of Mr Wesley's preachers at his death.[53]

Berridge thought that irregular methods were far better than no methods at all, and cared not if they gave offence to the idle, worldly-minded men who held the livings all around him. Thus a vicar who had left his college to live in an obscure out-of-the-way village shook the country near by, and was one of those who turned the world upside down. After his death Charles Simeon, in one of his Conversation Parties, made the comment: 'He was perhaps right in preaching from place to place as he did; but I who knew him well was hardly satisfied that he was doing right.[54] But that was not the whole story, for no one knew better than Simeon that times had changed; perhaps he felt that the mild hint of blame in his remark was not quite fair, for he went on to add a more generous appraisal:

> He lived when few ministers cared about the gospel and when disorder was almost needful. I don't think he would do now as he did then, for there are so many means of hearing the gospel, and a much greater spread of it; a much greater call for order, and much less need of disorder.[55]

It was men like Grimshaw in the North and Berridge in the Midlands who proved to be the salt that kept some real savour in the Church of England when Whitefield and Wesley burst the bounds of strict Church Order once and for all.

Berridge soon found that his labours in other men's vineyards provoked both opposition and persecution. A few of his converts were roughly handled, and their personal possessions were destroyed; gentry and clergy made common cause to check his progress and to halt his preaching. Complaints were laid before his college and his Bishop, and for thirty years he was commonly known as 'the Old Devil'.[56] He told David Simpson in 1775:

When I began to itinerate a multitude of dangers surrounded me and seemed ready to engulph me. My relations and friends were up in arms; my College was provoked; my Bishop incensed; the Clergy on fire; and the Church Canons pointing their ghastly mouths at me…. Then I saw if I meant to itinerate, I must not confer with flesh and blood, but cast myself wholly on the Lord. By His help, I did so, and made a surrender of myself to Jesus, expecting to be deprived not only of my Fellowship and Vicarage, but also of my liberty… But through the good blessing of my God, I am yet in possession of my senses, my tithes, and my liberty; and He Who hitherto delivered I trust will yet deliver me from the mouth of ecclesiastical lions and the paws of worldly bears. I have suffered from nothing except from lapidations and from pillory threats which yet have proved more frightful than hurtful.[57]

Neither threats nor acts of persecution ever kept him silent or made him inactive even for a single day in his long course of labour. A fair illustration is found in a letter to John Thornton on September 21, 1775:

Itinerant preaching affords me only one spare day in the week, and sometimes I am so jaded with riding and preaching that I seem fit for nothing on that spare day but to catch wasps, kill gnats, and count my teeth…. Oh dear Sir, every year makes me more ashamed of my worthless self! Eternity is just at hand, yet how lazy and lifeless I seem! Lord, quicken me![58]

If he defied Church Order with consistency, he also defied it with impunity. He held that most preachers love a snug church and a whole skin, and what they loved, they would prescribe. But if they were prepared to be irregular for the honour of Christ and the gospel, they would raise a storm in every quarter.[59] Berridge himself appeared not to know the meaning of fear, and was not in the least daunted either when faced with hostile crowds or with other dangers. Many of his escapades had an amusing side to them which must have helped to disarm opposition; it was inborn with that streak of quaintness which formed one part of his mental constitution. Charles Simeon told one of his Conversation Parties that he was once sent for by the Bishop and was reproved for his preaching at all hours of the day on all days of the week. 'My Lord,' Berridge replied, 'I preach only at two times.' And the Bishop inquired: 'Which are they, Mr Berridge?' And back came the reply: 'In season and out of season, my Lord.'[60] There was another occasion when he promised that in future he would refrain from his preaching tours in other livings, but he was soon arraigned for the same old breach of order. He found himself once more on the episcopal carpet, but he maintained that he had kept strictly to his promise. But one of the parishioners who lived on the edge of his own parish had asked him to come and preach to the men whom he employed and had offered him a wagon as a pulpit for the purpose. Berridge had not thought it amiss when he found the wagon stationed in a field close to the hedge which was in fact one of the parish boundaries; for he saw a crowd of people in the next field waiting to hear the Word of Life, and he could not find it in his heart to send them away merely because the field where they stood and waited was not on his side of the hedge.[61]

The most picturesque episode took place either at the close of the year 1759 or in the autumn of the year 1761. Only a year before his death Berridge told the story to a friend from Olney, through whom it was sent on to the *Evangelical Magazine*. When his church was filled with people from the neighbouring villages, other clergy were hurt to find their own churches empty; one of his own parishioners was also much annoyed, because he was incommoded by the presence of so many strangers. The laymen and clergy conspired to turn him out of his living, and had him brought before the Bishop of Lincoln on a charge of having preached out of his parish. He did not care for the summons, but he obeyed and was received in a very abrupt manner. 'Well, Berridge, they tell me you go about preaching out of your own parish,' said the Bishop. 'Did I institute you to the Livings of Abbotsley, or Eaton, or Potton?' 'No, my Lord,' he replied; 'neither do I claim any of these Livings; the clergymen enjoy them undisturbed by me.' 'Well, but you go and preach there,' the Bishop answered, 'which you have no right to do.' 'It is true, my Lord,' said Berridge. 'I was one day at Eaton, and there were a few poor people assembled together, and I admonished them to repent of their sins and to believe in the Lord Jesus Christ for the salvation of their souls; and I remember seeing five or six clergymen that day, my Lord, all out of their own parishes on Eaton Bowling Green.' 'Poh!' said His Lordship, 'I tell you, you have no right to preach out of your own parish, and if you do not desist from it, you will very likely be sent to Huntingdon Gaol.' 'As to that, my Lord,' he said, 'I have no greater liking to Huntingdon Gaol than other people; but I had rather go thither with a good conscience than live at my liberty without one.' At this point the Bishop looked hard at him, and then gravely said that he was beside himself and would soon be either better or worse. Berridge replied that if he were better in the Bishop's sense of the word, he would cease from preaching; and if worse, then Bedlam would do as well as the county gaol.[62]

But the Bishop changed his mode of attack, for he began, not to threaten, but to entreat. 'Berridge,' said he, 'you know I have been your friend, and I wish to be so still. I am continually teased with the complaints of the clergymen around you. Only assure me that you will keep to your own parish; you may do as you please there. I have but little time to live; do not bring down my grey hairs with sorrow to the grave.' Fortunately for the hapless Berridge, the names of two gentry were then sent in with a special request, and he was sent off to his inn with an invitation to come back for dinner. He went into a room and fell down on his knees; he could bear threats, but he knew not how to resist the pleas of an old man. On his return he dined with the Bishop and his two guests; then His Lordship took him outside and asked if he had thought out his request. 'I have, my Lord,' he said, 'and I have been on my knees concerning it.' 'Well,' said the Bishop, 'and will you promise me that you will preach no more out of your own parish?' 'It would afford me great pleasure', Berridge replied, 'to comply with Your Lordship's request, if I could do it with a good conscience. I am satisfied the Lord has blessed my labours of this kind, and I dare not desist.' 'A good conscience!' said the Bishop; 'do you know that it is contrary to the canons of the Church?' But this evoked the one crucial statement of the whole interview: 'There is one Canon, my Lord, which saith: Go, preach the gospel to every creature.' 'But why should you wish to interfere with the charge of other men?' asked the Bishop; 'one man cannot preach the gospel to all men.' 'If they would preach the gospel themselves,' he said, 'there would be no need for my preaching it to their people; but as they do not, I cannot desist.' Berridge then went home, not knowing what might befall, but most thankful to have kept his conscience inviolate. But then, unknown to him, an old friend and Fellow of Clare wrote to Thomas Pitt, the nephew of Lord Chatham, who went to the peer to whom the Bishop owed his See; the peer then saw the Bishop, who was compelled to leave Berridge unmolested in his labours. The Bishop of Lincoln had to inform the Squire of the failure of his summons, and when the Squire was asked if he had got the Old Devil out, he had to reply: 'No; nor do I think the very devil himself can get him out.'[63]

But what impact did such preaching make in Cambridge circles? Berridge possessed mental gifts and powers which had won him the highest reputation as a Fellow of Clare; he had strength of understanding, depth of penetration, a quick insight, and bright fancy, coupled with a fund of prompt wit beyond the lot of most. He was inferior to very few of the best-known sons of Cambridge in learning and letters in his own day, and he was widely known for his masculine intellect and his uniform excellence.[64] But these were gifts which he would not only count but loss for Christ's sake; he was all too ready to treat them with disdain as an active hindrance to the gospel. He once wrote:

> I studied the Classics, Mathematics, Philosophy, Logic,
> Metaphysics, and read the works of our most eminent
> divines; and this I did for twenty years; and all the while
> was departing more and more from the truth as it is in Jesus,
> vainly hoping to receive that light and instruction from
> human wisdom which could only be had from the Word of
> God and prayer.[65]

His own reaction was to abandon all the studies of his early
manhood, and shut himself up to one Book; and this course
he also sought to impress on his friends and converts, to the
chagrin of John Wesley, who wrote in April 1760:

> It seems to me that of all the persons I ever knew save one
> you are the hardest to be convinced. I have occasionally
> spoken to you on many heads, some of a speculative, others
> of a practical nature; but I do not know that you were ever
> convinced of one, whether of great importance or small. I
> believe you retained your own opinion in every one, and
> did not vary a hair's breadth…And this may be one reason
> why you take one step which was scarce ever before taken
> in Christendom—I mean the discouraging the new converts
> from reading—at least from reading anything but the Bible.
> Nay, but get off the consequence who can; if they ought to
> read nothing but the Bible, they ought to hear nothing but the
> Bible; so away with sermons, whether written or spoken![66]

But this contempt for the culture of the old world went hand
in hand with his new-born zeal to rule him out of favour in
the Cambridge circles where he had once been so welcome. He
was perhaps the first member of the University to be touched
by what was then called Enthusiasm, and the Fellows of Clare
were glad to see him leave in spite of the fact that he had formed
no college party. In November 1759 he was summoned as the
Select Preacher for the series of four sermons which were
delivered in Great St. Mary's. Wesley's journal for Monday,
November 26, contains a brief record of what transpired at the
final sermon:

In the evening Mr Berridge returned from preaching before the University. In the midst of the sermon, he informed me, one person cried out loud, but was silent in a few moments. Several dropped down, but made no noise, and the whole congregation, young and old, behaved with seriousness. God is strong as well as wise! Who knows what work He may have to do here also?[67]

But the Master of Corpus thought it a sign of uncommon lenity that it was left without rebuke,[68] and Dyer said plainly that it 'gave great offence to the University'.[69] He was asked no more to preach in Great St. Mary's, but like Holcroft in the experience of the ejected Puritans one hundred years before, he stirred up the counties of which Cambridge was the centre by his preaching in barns and farm-houses. His own parish was too far off for him to bring sustained pressure to bear on the students, but his contacts with the student world were kept green by his regular ministry at Grantchester. This small village marked the outer limit of his itinerant labours and was only a mile across the fields from the Backs of Cambridge. It was through his preaching in the fields at Grantchester that he at length made his finest contact with the students, and did so much to form the views of some of these young men in the later 'sixties.

In October 1764 Rowland Hill was entered as a Freshman at St. John's, and his name came to Berridge as that of a fearless witness to Christ. Berridge promptly sent him a note on December 18:

> I am now at Grantchester, a mile from you...where I shall abide till three in the afternoon; will you take a walk over?...If you love Jesus Christ, you will not be surprised at this freedom taken with you by a stranger who seeks your acquaintance only out of his love to Christ and His people.[70]

Rowland Hill rode over and met him as proposed, and thus set on foot a friendship of great charm and beauty. From that day forth he made it his habit to ride to Everton week by week on Sunday, and to return in time for chapel in St. John's. Seldom did the weather ever stand in his way, and he drank deep from the thought and experience of one whom he looked upon as an old soldier. He spent his first Christmas recess at Everton, and soon formed a society for his friends in Cambridge somewhat on the model of the Holy Club at Oxford. He was able to get some ten or twelve fellow students to meet for the study of the Greek Text of the New Testament, and they were soon taken to the Everton Vicarage to meet Berridge himself. Rowland Hill began to visit the sick and those in gaol, and to preach in private homes in and around Cambridge. Sidney declares that there never was a leader more widely loved or more gladly followed by his fellow students than was Rowland Hill in Cambridge.[71] He excelled in athletic exercise, and he took his degree in January 1769 with a high place on the list of honours. With birth, rank, and a fortune, in the background, with sport, charm, and culture in the foreground, he seemed to have all that a young man might wish for; and there were none whom he loved or honoured more than Whitefield and Berridge. The six students who were expelled from St. Edmund Hall at Oxford in March 1768 on the ground of friendship with men like Henry Venn and John Fletcher were a warning of the troubles which he might encounter, but he never faltered in his witness to Christ or in his love for His servants.

But he was not without his trials. On his graduation, no less than six bishops in turn refused to ordain him, and it only remained for Berridge to counsel him 'to stand still and not to hurry'.[72] But he would not have him desist from his itinerant preaching through fear that he might miss ordination; he urged him to keep up all his irregular labours for the love of Christ and the souls of men. 'Be not anxious about Orders; they will come as soon as wanted,' he wrote in January 1770; 'nor be anxious about anything but to know the Lord's will and to do the Lord's work.'[73] Rowland Hill had to wait on in patience, but his labours would have damped all the zeal of the less energetic. Then a further letter in May 1771 came to cheer him.

Dear Rowly, My heart sends you some of its kindest love and breathes its tenderest wishes for you. I feel my heart go out to you whilst I am writing, and can embrace you as my second self. How soft and sweet are those silken cords which the dear Redeemer twines and ties about the hearts of His children!...Go forth my dear Rowly wherever you are invited into the devil's territories; carry the Redeemer's standard along with you; and blow the gospel trumpet boldly, fearing nothing but yourself...Now is your time to work for Jesus; you have health and youth on your side, and no church or wife on your back.[74]

At length, on June 6, 1773, he was ordained by the Bishop of Bath and Wells without condition or restriction of any kind; but he never took Priest's Orders, and he never held a regular benefice in the Church of England. Berridge described him as 'a comet' whose path was eccentric and unconfined, and he was charmed by his constant activity.[75] On September 3, 1773 he wrote: 'Avoid all controversy in preaching, talking, or writing; preach nothing down but the devil, and nothing up but Jesus Christ.'[76] Rowland Hill could never forget his debt to this friendship; he paid a most loving tribute to the good old hero after his death.

Many a mile have I rode, many a storm have I faced, many a snow have I gone through to hear good old Mr Berridge; for I felt his ministry when in my troubles at Cambridge a comfort and blessing to my soul. Dear affectionate old man, I loved him to my heart.[77]

Berridge grew in friendship with Whitefield and Wesley from the first days of the Everton Revival, but the Calvinistic controversy was to draw him to the one more than the other. In February 1761 and January 1762 Wesley preached in his church, and found that the congregation had grown much more settled with a steady increase of the work of God in their souls.[78] In the same two months Whitefield wrote that Berridge had been preaching for him in the Tabernacle 'like an angel of light' and 'with great flame'.[79] But his personal relations with Wesley were slightly awkward from the spring of 1760, for Wesley's autocratic spirit was disturbed by his rustic independence.[80] This was aggravated by the change in his views on the Doctrines of Grace, a change which came to a head in 1768 when he was laid aside by a nervous fever. He had been a rigid Arminian, but it amazed him to see how the work of God went on in his absence. Venn was greatly surprised at his growth in unaffected humility and sweetness of temper as a result of that illness, and it seems to have led him to embrace the full Doctrines of Grace:[81]

> A furnace is the proper school to learn this doctrine in, and there I learnt it. Nor men nor books could teach it me, for I would neither hear nor read about it. A long and rancorous war I waged with it; and when my sword was broken and both my arms were maimed, I yet maintained a sturdy fight and was determined I would never yield; but a furnace quelled me. Large afflictions, largely wanted, gave me such experience of my evil heart that I could peep upon electing grace without abhorrence; and as I learnt to loathe myself, I learnt to prize this grace. It seemeth clear that if God had mercy for me, it could only be for this gracious reason, that He would have mercy.'[82]

This led to a breach with Wesley which the latter's *Letters* reflect with mild concern,[83] and which finds an echo in one of the few hard sayings found in Berridge: 'We are told that some very honest folks who are cast in a gospel-Foundery often ring a fire-bell to quench these very doctrines.'[84]

When the Calvinistic controversy broke out early in the 'seventies, Berridge was moved to an ill-starred attempt at the defence of his doctrines. Thus in 1773 he brought out a little treatise under the quaint title, *The Christian World Unmasked: Pray Come and Peep*. It was written in a rather rough-and-tumble style, though moderate in tone, and it plainly deplored the whole controversy. Berridge did not refer to Wesley or Fletcher by name at all, but their tenets were laughed at and attacked. It took the form of a dialogue between two imaginary characters as to the way of salvation. 'Gentle Reader,' it began, 'lend

me a chair, and I will sit down and talk a little with you.'[85] A faith
that floats on the surface like froth on the water is vain;[86] one
who is not a real subject of Christ must still be a stranger to
the blessings of His Kingdom.[87] It is clear and pointed when it
speaks of 'a sweet-heart sin'[88] or when it talks of grace as 'the
blossom bud of glory'.[89] It is plain and pithy when we read that
'where God gives repentance, it is never meant to purchase par-
don; for tears pay no debts'.[90] The good news falls upon dull ears
just like money dropping into the hand of a dead man; no good
comes from money or news because the dead have no value for
them.[91] But his gospel was as clear as a bell, and its sound is
heard in words that ring like a chime:

> Jesus Christ the Bread of Life is freely offered in the gospel
> to every hungry famished soul. Such are prepared for the
> bread, and the bread prepared for such. And these should
> never pore upon the Doctrine of Election, but muse upon
> the gospel promises and call on Jesus confidently to fulfil
> them. He turns no real beggar from His gate, though full of
> sores and vermin. His heart is lined with sweet compassion
> and His hands are stored with gifts. He has supplies for all
> wants...and a rope for a sham beggar who asks for mercy
> and yet talks of merit![92]

Who would not add their glad 'Amen' to a declaration of the
gospel so free and so simple?

But he was too loving for acrimony, and he had no real heart
for controversy; the duel had no sooner begun than he wished
himself out of it. On August 31, 1773 he wrote to John Thornton:

> Whatever Mr Fletcher may write against my pamphlet,
> I am determined to make no reply. I dare not trust my own
> wicked heart in a controversy. If my pamphlet is faulty, let
> it be overthrown; if sound, it will rise up above any learned
> rubbish that is cast upon it.[93]

He had grown weary of the self-imposed task while it was being
carried out, and he was quite sick of it since it had been finished.

On September 25 he wrote again: 'I have wrote to Mr Fletcher and told him...I was afraid that Mr Toplady and himself were setting the Christian world on fire...and wished they could both desist from controversy!'[94] But he could not settle his own score out of court, and he was quite out-matched when the *Answer* appeared. Fletcher indeed seems to have thought that his desire to drop the whole controversy sprang more from fear of his pen than from love of peace, but he paid a magnanimous tribute to his vital piety and his tireless energy for the gospel. On March 1, 1774 Fletcher's Answer came from the press with the title, *Logica Genivensis Continued*, or *The Second Part to the Fifth Check to Antinomianism*.

> Before I mention Mr Berridge's mistakes, I must do justice to his person...His conduct as a Christian is exemplary; his labours as a minister are great; and I am persuaded that the wrong touches which he gives to the ark of godliness are not only undesigned, but intended to do God service. There are so many things commendable in the pious Vicar of Everton and so much truth in his Christian World Unmasked that I find it a hardship to expose the unguarded parts of that performance.[95]

> I only do him justice when I say that few, very few of our elders equal him in devotedness to Christ, zeal, diligence, and ministerial success. His indefatigable labours in the Word and doctrine entitle him to a double share of honour, and I invite all my readers to esteem him highly in love for his Master's and his work's sake.[96]

Berridge had had enough of the controversy, and he frankly owned that there were difficulties in the case which defied the power of man's reason to solve. He made up his mind to adhere to one leading maxim, namely that Man's Salvation is all of God while Man's Destruction is of himself.[97] When an eminent minister asked him whether he had read this and that on the controversy, he made reply: 'I have them on my shelves in my library where they are very quiet; if I take them down and look into them, they will begin to quarrel and disagree.'[98] It is often stated that Fletcher and Berridge had not met since the year 1760 when they had been of the same mind on all points of doctrine.[99] But this is not correct; for in August 1770 they had both been present at the meetings which were held to celebrate the first anniversary of the College at Trevecca.[100] But in December 1776 Fletcher paid his second visit to the Everton Vicarage, and proved that there was no room for rancour in hearts like theirs. Berridge ran to meet him as he came through the door, embraced him with both arms, and hailed him as 'my dear brother!'[101] Never perhaps did two spirits of more kindred joy meet with each other, and for two hours they were absorbed in most affectionate conversation. Then they took to their knees, while each joined in prayer of the most warm and tender spirit; it seemed almost as if they could not bear to part, and had to tear themselves away so that Fletcher could meet Venn at St. Neots. Not many months later, in the spring of 1777, Berridge was in London, and planned to meet Fletcher at Stoke Newington; we do not know any details of this meeting, except that it was in love and goodwill.[102] Charles Simeon told a story at one of his Conversation Parties from which it is clear that he and Venn took Fletcher with them to see Berridge at least once more; and this must have been at some point between the year 1782, when Berridge first met Simeon, and the year 1785, when Fletcher died at Madeley.[103] 'Grace makes the heart gracious', as Berridge said; it plants benevolence where self would reign.[104]

This one work on controversy was almost his only literary contribution, though he also published a book of hymns. But he was no more a poet than was Cromwell, and his private letters were worth far more than his *Songs of Zion*. The 'Twenty Six Sermon Outlines' which found their way into his *Works* give us only a faint idea of his talent as a preacher. They are very simple, full of Scripture, deeply spiritual; but they contain nothing very deep or striking, nothing really quaint or original. But when he stood in the pulpit, his brief 'Outlines' were clothed with new vitality. He would seldom refer to the notes which he had prepared, but on the spur of the moment he would bring in a host of fresh ideas. His style was plain, colloquial at times, evangelical in thought, experimental in thrust, with words that were meant to strike the understanding of the dullest hearer. There was a vast store of racy anecdote and whimsical illustration; there was no end to his homely narrative and humorous application. The rich vein of guileless humour which ran through his sermons helped to soften the austerities of Truth, while it never upset his own sense of gravity or of dignity; others might seem lost in laughter, but he was in perfect control. His grand aim was to make men grasp his point, and to achieve that aim he was content to let other things go. Pithy comments and quaint asides might make men smile, but they kept them awake; he might break the canons of taste, but what was that if hearts were broken too? Better a thousand times to make men smile and get them saved than to leave them looking stiff and grave and formal, without grace or blessing, in the pews where they sat.[105] There have been few preachers in the Church of England who have better known how to get into vital touch with the plough-boy mind,[106] and there can be no doubt that he stands high in the line of preachers who look back to old Hugh Latimer for a certain tang of rustic power and popular homeliness.[107]

There were sometimes ten or fifteen thousand who stood to hear him in the fields, and some who came from a distance would set out soon after midnight to reach the church in time for the service which he held at seven in the morning. He preached again at ten o'clock, at half-past two, and in the evening, and he hardly ever preached in vain.[108] Numbers would wait on him to ask how they were to be saved, and they would not return home without an answer. At first he kept a list of the names and dwellings of all who thus applied to him, and the first year of his gospel preaching brought a thousand people to his door in profound spiritual concern.[109] His heart went out in love and strong desire for his hearers, and he strove to provide for their needs in body as well as in spirit. His own tables at home were served with a cold meal for those who had come from afar, while his field and stable were free for their horses; away from home, cottage folk would always receive a half-crown for the homely fare set before him, and this item alone cost him no less than £500 in his long career as an itinerant preacher.[110] He had to hire barns at his own expense so that converts could meet without trouble, and three times at least he found the money for the erection of a permanent meeting-place for their benefit.[111] He had perforce to become the patron of a small band of lay preachers to shepherd his converts, and their needs had to be met from his own pocket. His own habits were simple and frugal in the extreme, but the income from his Fellowship, his Benefice, his patrimony, and even from the sale of his family plate were all used up in the service of souls. In January 1766 Romaine told Lady Huntingdon of his heavy expense,[112] and she sent him £15 to help clothe his lay preachers.[113] But when he had nothing of his own he used to apply to John Thornton, and he never seems to have asked in vain; letters to John Thornton all through the 'seventies are full of gratitude for the books and money which he received for the sake of others.[114]

'Of all the Evangelists of the Eighteenth Century', wrote Ryle, 'this good man was undeniably the most quaint and eccentric.'[115] He was naturally mercurial in mind and thought, a man *sui generis*, one who had to stand in a class by himself, one who said and did things which no one else could do or say. He had gifts of intellect of the highest order combined with a keen sense for the odd and the ludicrous, and his mind was cast in such a mould that he could not help putting things in the most piquant manner. He had once soaked himself in the works of Samuel Butler and of Aristophanes, and was famous as a wit and humorist; and this flair for the quaint was in his bones, it was part and parcel of his mental constitution.[116] In October 1775 Thornton found fault with a phrase in his prayer that God would give new bread, not stale, bread that had been baked and came fresh from the oven that day. 'I remember', wrote Thornton, 'you once jocularly informed me you were born with a fool's cap on; pray, my dear Sir, is it not high time it was pulled off?' But he replied: 'A very proper question; and my answer is this—a fool's cap is not put off so readily as a night cap; one cleaves to the head, and the other to the heart.'[117] But if the grace of God in him were like champagne in a vessel of clay, better surely an excess of quaintness than excess of dullness! His wit never hurt a soul in trouble, nor hardened a sinner in impenitence; it may have mortified the all too complacent, and it would not suffer the drones to sleep. And quaint as his sayings so often were, one can seldom fail to discern in them that shrewd sagacity which always tells. Nor was he unconscious of his own eccentric turn of thought. 'Oh heart, heart, what art thou?' he wrote in July 1763; 'A mass of fooleries and absurdities! The vainest, foolishest, craftiest, wickedest thing in nature. And yet the Lord Jesus asks me for this heart, woos me for it, died to win it. O wonderful love! Adorable condescension! Take it Lord, and let it be Ever closed to all but Thee.'[118]

Berridge was tall and graceful in bearing, pleasant though solemn in address, with a clear and deep voice which could be heard by the largest crowd as well as Whitefield's.[119] In his early prime, the Senior Fellow of Clare, popular companion, famous wit, and brilliant scholar, must have been an attractive bachelor. But his relatives and old companions left him in the lurch when he took his stand for the gospel, and he had some thought of marriage at the time when he first went to reside in the Everton Vicarage. His housekeepers were a torment to him, so he betook himself to prayer. The rest of the story is best told in his own words to Lady Huntingdon:

> Falling down on my knees before a table with a Bible between my hands, I besought the Lord to give me a direction; then letting the Bible fall open of itself, I fixed my eyes immediately on these words, 'When my son was entered into his wedding chamber, he fell down and died' (2 Esdras 10: 1). This frightened me heartily, you may easily think; but Satan who stood peeping at my elbow, not liking the heavenly caution, presently suggested a scruple that the Book was apocryphal, and the words not to be heeded. Well,

after a short pause, I fell on my knees again and prayed the Lord not to be angry with me whilst like Gideon I requested a second sign, and from the Canonical Scripture; then letting my Bible fall open as before, I fixed my eyes directly on this passage: 'Thou shalt not take thee a wife, neither shalt thou have sons or daughters in this place' (Jer. 16: 2). I was now completely satisfied![120]

He would not leave his faith buried beneath mountains when it ought to move them, and he readily accepted this as the sign for which he had made bold to ask. But his eccentric turn of character was never so clearly revealed as in the attitude which he now adopted. 'No trap so mischievous to the field-preacher as wedlock,' he told Lady Huntingdon, 'and it is laid for him at every hedge corner. Matrimony has quite maimed poor Charles [Wesley], and might have spoiled John [Wesley] and George [Whitefield] if a wise Master had not graciously sent them a brace of ferrets.'[121]

But he was a man of warm and generous affections, and he never lacked for friendship. He was always a favourite with Lady Huntingdon, and she often asked him to her London home to meet the great and courtly. In 1761 she induced him to take charge of her Brighton Chapel for a few weeks;[122] in 1767 she secured his choice with that of Venn and Fletcher as a chaplain to the Earl of Buchan.[123] He was wont to visit London each year in the winter from soon after Christmas till just before Easter, when he would preach to great congregations in the Tabernacle and the Tottenham Court Chapel; but this yearly visit was the only time when he was willing to go out of his own district, and more than one letter to the Countess was a humorous refusal of her pressing invitations. Thus on November 16, 1762 he wrote:

> I cannot see my call to Brighthelmstone; and I ought to see it for myself, not another for me. Was any good done when I was there? It was God's doing; all the glory be to Him. This shows I did not then go without my Master, but is no proof of a second call.[124]

Or on December 26, 1767:

> Verily you are a good piper, but I know not how to dance.
> I love your scorpion letters dearly, though they rake the flesh
> off my bones; and I believe your eyes are better than my own,
> but I cannot yet read with your glasses. I do know that I want
> quickening every day, but I do not see that I want a journey
> to Bath.'[125]

He said that when he left his bees to go abroad, it was only to
find when he came home that the air was full of useless buzzing
when they should be winning honey from all the flowers
in God's garden.[126] 'A gospel minister who has a church will
have a diocese annexed to it,' he wrote, 'and let him like faithful
Grimshaw look well to it.'[127] But he never forgot his debt to her,
and he honoured her to the end. 'Mrs. Carteret…tells me I owe
you a letter,' he wrote in April 1777. 'Your Ladyship might tell Mrs.
Carteret I owe you much love, which will ever be paying, I trust,
and never be paid.'[128] On news of her death in 1791 he quietly
said: 'Ah! is she dead? Then another pillar is gone to glory.'[129]

Perhaps Henry Venn was of all his friends the one he knew
longest and loved the most, for their friendship went back to their
Cambridge days and endured till death. He was greatly cheered
when Venn was installed in the nearby church at Yelling, and
the winter months of 1771 were marked by a monthly exchange
of each other's pulpit. Thus on November 22, 1771 Venn wrote:
'Last Wednesday Mr Berridge was here, and gave us a most
excellent sermon.'[130] Or on December 7, 1773 we read: 'Dear
Mr Berridge preaches for me every month; happy am I in having
such a loving, fervent minister of Christ!'[131] Berridge was soon
engaged in getting his support for field and barn preaching, and
in August 1774 he told Thornton:

> I have been recruiting for Mr Venn at Godmanchester, a very
> populous and wicked town near Huntingdon, and met with
> a patient hearing from a numerous audience. I hope he also
> will consecrate a few barns, and preach a little in his neigh-
> bourhood to fill up his fold at Yelling.…I tell my brother he

need not fear being hanged for sheep-stealing while he only whistles the sheep to a better pasture and meddles neither with the flesh nor fleece.[132]

In August 1776 Venn wrote: 'Mr Berridge is in London; he laboured for three months above his strength. He had the largest congregations that were ever known for a constancy, and greatly was his word owned of the Lord. He is as affectionate as a father to my son, and gives him many valuable books.'[133] In June 1778 Berridge wrote to Thornton: 'Young Venn is the most promising youth I have seen; great mental abilities, close application to study, and much unction from the Holy One.'[134] In October 1778 he wrote: 'I preached at Yelling on Tuesday evening to a large congregation, and left the family in good health. Jacky goes on well, is very studious and serious, and promises to be a polished shaft in the Lord's quiver.'[135] Berridge had lost touch with Cambridge life since the last of Rowland Hill's group of friends had gone down in 1771; he seems to have made up his mind that Cambridge did not breed the kind of men he wanted.[136] Henry Venn was to take his place as the guide and friend of Cambridge students, but for a while John Venn revived all his old interest with intense joy.

On June 14, 1782 John Venn took Charles Simeon with him to meet Berridge in his home at Everton; but his lode-star was to be with Henry Venn at Yelling, whom he went to visit six times within the next three months. Those three months had elapsed before Berridge mentioned his name for the first time in one of his letters, and that letter was more interested in John Venn whom it describes as 'a very gracious youth'.[137] But in 1785 Henry Venn was preaching in a barn for a young farmer named Coxe Feary at Bluntisham; he met with such marks of success in this Fenland village that he promised to preach once a fortnight on his return from his summer visit to Rowland Hill's Surrey Chapel. Simeon rode over from Cambridge each Sunday to preach at Yelling while he was away; then he agreed at the urgent request of John Berridge to preach at Bluntisham as well. Thus for three Sundays he preached at Cambridge in the morning, at Yelling in the afternoon, and in a barn at Bluntisham in the evening. But when Henry Venn heard of his visits to this barn in the Fens, he wrote at once to say how grieved he was at his conduct; grieved, as Berridge remarked, at his doing what he himself had done, and meant to do! But Venn carried the day and there was no more barn preaching for him, in spite of new entreaties from the flock at Bluntisham. Berridge poured out his own disappointment in a letter to John Thornton on July 2, 1785: 'Yelling Church is well attended under Mr Simeon's afternoon ministry. A brave Christian Sargeant he is, having the true spirit of an Evangelist; but his feet are often put into the stocks by the Archdeacon of Yelling who is doubtless become a vagabond preacher as well as myself, a right gospel hawker and pedlar, but seems desirous of having the trade to himself. Through mercy he is grown as scandalous as I could wish him, yet he wants to fasten the shackles on Simeon which he has dropped from himself.... Mr Venn is grieved at his conduct, grieved at Simeon for doing what himself had done, and intended to do. This surely is grief of all griefs, and too deep even for tragedy. Pray, Sir, lay your cane soundly on the Archdeacon's back when you see him and brush off this heathen grief, else it may spoil a Christian Sargeant.'[138]

Berridge had made Rowland Hill a lifelong itinerant, a copy of himself in passion for souls, in humour of speech, in disregard for Church Order, and as irregular as he ever had been; and he would have done the same for Simeon but for Venn's emphatic intervention. Canon Smyth points out that one of the most decisive elements in the development of the Evangelical Party within the Church of England was this unshakable resolution on Venn's part that Simeon's ministry should not be robbed of its promise by such irregular preaching and scorn of Church Order. It was not that Venn had been so particular in his own life as an evangelist; he had largely learned from Berridge the way in which to make use of barns as 'threshing floors for Jesus'. But it was one thing for Venn and Berridge to preach in barns or fields to those who were left in neglect by their lawful pastors; they were old men, and their day was over. But it was quite a new story for a Cambridge vicar whose life was so rich in promise to go out of his own way to borrow customs when it would be so much better that they should die with them.[139] Thus Venn and Simeon were to do for Cambridge in the end the very thing that Berridge and Rowland Hill had tried, but failed, to do; and they were to do it by strict conformity to the order of the Church of England. But there was no rupture in the personal relations between friends of such true standing; Simeon told one of his Conversation Parties in later years how he and Venn used to go over and dine with Berridge every Tuesday.[140] After his death Venn wrote, on February 14, 1793, in terms of most wholehearted affection: He 'was most affectionate towards all my dear children, and his regard for me was very great indeed. His departure is to me a loss unspeakable, and not to be repaired. The country will appear very dreary now I have no friend there to whom I can unbosom my soul as he was wont to do to me.'[141] It is good to know that Rowland Hill, though himself wholly given to an itinerant apostolate, spoke with delight of Simeon, and would not preach in a place of Dissent while in Cambridge lest it should take away from his prestige with so many gownsmen.[142]

Berridge was not only never married, but he lived quite alone; and his parish was buried in the country in days when even turn-pike roads were full of troubles. He had settled in a county away from his family and their connections; he wrote very little, and was chiefly known to others by his preaching. He had thrown in his lot with a sect which all men spoke against, and we need not wonder that the records of his life are meagre. But his memoir was sketched by a former curate after his death, and more details may be found in the Letters and journals of his Evangelical contemporaries. He was a man of great kindness and rare unselfishness, as his own words unconsciously reveal: 'I...save all I can, to give all I can.'[143] He lived in a very frugal manner, and his labours for Christ cost him all that he had. There were prayers in his house at nine in the morning and nine in the evening; and on Saturday evenings the more godly in the village would join him at seven o'clock. It was profound necessity which had compelled him to preach Christ, and that made him willing to lose his life for the gospel if so be he might save it for ever. There were more than common shrewdness and good sense veiled behind many of his laughing comments; his critique of Cowper's Poems and his letters about Trevecca, the skilful candour in his statement on Calvinism and the balanced judgment in his treatment of Enthusiasts, all prove him to have been well taught in that wisdom which cometh from above. Robinson of Leicester used to cite the reverence of Everton as a model proof of what the Church of England could be in its worship.[144] His constant theme as a preacher is well portrayed in a letter of January 1766 to Lady Margaret, in which the Robe of Righteousness is offered thus: 'It was wrought with My own hand and dyed with My own blood; wear it, and remember Me.'[145] His simple faith as a sinner is then revealed in a letter of December 1767 to Lady Huntingdon, in which he says: 'A robe I must have, of one whole piece, broad as the Law, spotless as the Light, and richer than an angel ever wore—the robe of Jesus.'[146] No one could have been more alert to his infirmities or more conscious of his need in spirit. 'I am now sinking from a poor something into a vile nothing,' he wrote in 1773, 'and I wish to be nothing that Christ may be all.'[147]

Berridge was cheerful and pleasant in manner just as he was humble and gracious in spirit. 'Sir, I have known Mr Berridge above forty years,' said an old man after his death and the sermon that was preached in London, 'and...I must say as the Queen of Sheba did respecting Solomon, the half has not been told.'[148] Would we learn how he took the Word of God for the comfort of his own soul? We hear him say:

> Though He slay me, yet will I trust Him, that is, I will not let Him go. This is the language of the church in the deepest distress. In ourselves, we are certainly lost; how the Lord will deal with us we know not. We see not our signs or tokens any more; yet we will lay ourselves down at His feet and pray...

And this sometimes proves an anchor to a tossed soul, which though it brings not peace, yet saves from despair. Here faith rests till more light breaks forth.[149]

Would we know how he used the Word of God for the comfort of other men?

The pen may well be compared to the ministers of the gospel. It seems they have been trying for many years to make good pens at the universities; but after all the ingenuity and pains taken, the pens which are made there are good for nothing till God has nibbed them!…The nib…I compare to the influence of Divine Grace upon the heart…Lift up your hearts in prayer for the poor pen and say, Lord, give him a little more ink!…In all these Epistles, there must be somewhat written: Repentance is written with a broad-nibbed pen in the old black letter of the Law at the foot of Mount Sinai. Faith is written with a crow-quill pen in fine and gentle strokes at the foot of Mount Calvary.[150]

We may hear him hit off Bashfulness as 'a fair-faced slip of pride', in his letter to John Thornton in September 1775; but he goes on to add with the insight that sees into the heart of things: 'The forward and the bashful temper are contraries, yet both originate from the same source. One pushes forward in hope of showing itself to advantage; the other lags behind for fear of appearing to disadvantage.'[151]

Berridge had put great strain on his health and physique by his mode of life in constant journeys and long hours of preaching in all weathers, year in, year out, ever since the Everton Revival. It would appear from one of his letters that his first real setback occurred in June 1768, when high fever laid him by for five months; this was followed by a nervous fever which clung to him for some five years. He said in June 1771:

In the winter, I am somewhat braced and can make a poor shift to preach on the Sabbath, but nothing more. As soon as the hot weather comes in, I am fit for nothing but to sigh and yawn. Last summer I did not preach for four months…

and how much longer I shall be able to preach, I know not. My breast is so weak that I can bear very little exercise... and I am so tender that I cannot stir out of doors in summer without a cloak when there is a wind.'[152]

Five days later he told Lady Huntingdon: 'My health and strength are declining apace since the warm weather came in. My legs are almost gone, and my horse is almost useless. As yet I have been able to do whole duty on the Sabbath, but fear I shall be laid up soon. Do my dear Lady wrestle with me in prayer that I may be strengthened to labour, and get the men and women of Israel to help.'[153] Henry Venn bears this out in a letter of November 1771: 'Summer differs not more from winter than this dear man from what he was ten years ago.'[154] But in June 1773 Berridge could write: 'My health through mercy is much better than it has been for five years.'[155] He resumed his labours, and his sense of humour kept him cheerful. Thus Venn still found him a model in all that had to do with God, and in August 1776 he wrote: 'His life is a pattern to us all, and an incitement to love and serve the Lord with all our strength.'[156] In December 1780 he told Newton of a vicar who had asked him to preach, and laughingly observed: 'Indeed, he is a bold man to ask the mad-man of Everton to dust his cushion!' Then he went on to say: 'The Lord...has strengthened my body for itinerant preaching the last three months, and is crowding my church abundantly on a Sunday afternoon. Glory be to His grace!'[157]

Thus he maintained his full round of activities in the 'eighties, though Venn observed in December 1 782 that his voice was losing its power.[158] In July 1785 Berridge told Thornton: 'My church is usually very full in afternoons and the people are awake and attentive, but the congregation is almost a new one. Many old sheep are housed in the upper fold, and many who live at a distance are dropped into neighbouring meetings.'[159] But three months of illness ensued, and two Sundays at least he could not preach.[160] In October 1787 he found his health improved, but his faculties had begun to fail.[161] In February 1788 he grew weary of his stay in London and felt a new longing for Everton where he would have leisure to muse upon the Word of God in prayer. 'Never am I well', he said, 'but when at home with Jesus.'[162] In the 'nineties he was old and feeble, very solitary, with no wife or sister to care for him, but strong in peace and much in prayer. He had to do less and less in public, and he suffered much at times from curious forms of delusion. 'His sight is very dim,' wrote Venn in 1791, 'his ears can scarcely hear, and his faculties are fast decaying, so that if he continues any time he may outlive the use of them. But in this ruin of his earthly tabernacle, it is surprising to see the joy in his countenance.' Venn was moved to hear him pray as if he were quite alone; 'but if I have Thy presence and love, that sufficeth!'[163] In August 1792 Berridge wrote, it would seem, to Venn's eldest daughter: 'The two last Sundays I was led to church and into the pulpit; my voice was feeble, but hearable, and Christ was precious.'[164] In January, 1793 on the very morning when he meant to set out on his yearly visit to London, he was rendered prostrate by a violent asthmatic attack, and from that hour his strength began visibly, rapidly, to wane. On Sunday January 20 he was carried downstairs for the last time, for he only reached his bedroom in the evening with great difficulty. 'Jesus will soon call you up higher,' someone said, and he whispered in reply: 'Aye, aye, aye, higher, higher, higher!'[165] Within a few hours worse symptoms appeared, and then his speech began to fail. He had seldom spoken but in terms of love and adoration, and Venn says that he was 'unspeakably favoured with the presence and love' of his Saviour.[166] At length, at three o'clock on Tuesday afternoon, January 22, the weary wheels of life stood still, and at 75 years of age, without struggle or groan, the good old man slept safe in the arms of Jesus.

Bibliography

Richard Whittingham, *The Works of The Rev. John Berridge, A.M., with an enlarged Memoir of his Life* (1838), and an App-endix (1844).

John Charles Ryle, 'John Berridge and His Ministry', Chapter VIII in *Christian Leaders of the Last Century* (New Ed., 1880).

Nehemiah Curnock, *The Journal of The Rev. John Wesley, A.M.* (Bicentenary Issue, 1938).

John Telford, *The Letters of The Rev. John Wesley*, A.M. (Standard Ed., 1931).

Luke Tyerman, *The Life of The Rev. George Whitefield* (2nd Ed., 1890).

Luke Tyerman, *Wesley's Designated Successor* (1882).

'A Member of The Houses of Shirley and Hastings', *The Life and Times of Selina, Countess of Huntingdon* (1839).

John Venn and Henry Venn, *The Life and a Selection from the Letters of the late Rev. Henry Venn, M.A.* (1837).

Edwin Sidney, T*he Life of the Rev. Rowland Hill, A.M.* (1834)

Abner William Brown, *Recollections of The Conversation Parties of The Rev. Charles Simeon*, M.A. (1863).

Charles Smyth, *Simeon and Church Order* (1940).

G. R. Balleine, *A History of the Evangelical Party* (New Ed., 1933).

'I most gladly bear my testimony that not the half, nor the hundredth part of what might have been justly said of that blessed man of God is here spoken. If any person now living, his surviving children alone excepted, is qualified to bear this testimony, it is I; who from my first entrance into Orders to his dying hour, had most intimate access to him, and enjoyed most of his company and conversation. How great a blessing his conversation and example have been to me will never be known till the Day of judgment.'

Charles Simeon (see Life and Letters of Henry Venn, 55–6)

3

Henry Venn
1724–97

Henry Venn was born in the Surrey village of Barnes on March 2, 1724, the third of eight children who came to fill that home with love and laughter. All his paternal ancestors from the reign of Elizabeth down to his own time had been in Holy Orders in the Church of England, and he was to be the fifth in this long line of unbroken succession. They were High Church Clergy of the old school, and had won their mede of honour for piety and loyalty. His own father was a devout churchman who had become Rector of St. Antholin's in London, where he fought for the fair name of the English Church with learning and courage. In December 1733 he stood out in London against the choice of a Deist for the See of Gloucester, and spurned a bribe which was meant to keep him silent. In October 1737 he proved himself the first London rector to shut Whitefield out of his church, and to take up his pen against the Methodists.[1] But he died in the year 1739, at the early age of forty-eight leaving three sons and a daughter in his widow's care. Henry Venn was only a lad of fifteen at the time of his father's death, and the known facts of his childhood are few enough. But they show that he had a strength and decision of character, a force and energy of intellect, which were bound to give tone and distinction to his life as it developed. On one occasion when an Arian visitor came to see his father, the child gravely eyed him from head to foot. Friendly overtures were made to him, but were sternly repulsed. At length the visitor pressed him to come nearer, but was met with the indignant reply: 'I will not come near you, for you are an Arian!'[2] His father's London home was in the same street as the home of a Dissenting minister, whose son was two or three years older than himself; but his zeal for the Church made him feel no fear or scruple in waylaying and attacking the Dissenter's son whenever he could.[3] Loyalty to his father was synonymous with loyalty to the Church of England.

Such force of character was not without dangerous qualities; it was a power which might produce much good or much evil. Thus one of his father's friends once declared that in due time he would go to Holborn, and would either stop at the Palace of Ely or would go on to the gallows at Tyburn. He was first sent to school at the age of twelve, and he spent some two years at Mortlake near Barnes. Then he went to Fulham, but left soon after his father's death at his own request; he wanted to attend a school of stricter standards in learning and discipline! He spent twelve months at a school near Bristol, and twelve months more at a school in Market Street, Hertfordshire; he was in fact enrolled in this school in the same year in which William Cowper left it for Westminster after he had borne the tyranny which sank so deep into his mind.[4] Venn had been well grounded in the Classics, and was more than ready in June 1742, at the age of seventeen, to take his place in Cambridge. At first he joined his elder brother at St. John's College, but he transferred to Jesus College three months later when he was awarded a Rustat Scholarship. He took his Arts Degree in 1745, and was made a Scholar of his College in 1747; he was chosen as a Fellow of Queens' College in 1749, and was made a Master of Arts in the same year. He was soon surrounded by a large and pleasant circle of friends, and his company was much sought after by his fellow students. He had a rich fund of high spirits which made him the life and soul of any party; he had all the gifts of social grace which go to make an attractive companion. A vivacious manner, a mild and engaging temper, a mind stored with anecdote, a flair as a raconteur; these all were the gifts of nature, and were enhanced by his delicate courtesy and his genial affection. As a child he had been the favourite of his home and neighbourhood; as a student he was no less popular as a friend and companion. There were perhaps very few men then at Cambridge who were so widely loved or so truly esteemed.

In June 1747 he was ordained by the Bishop of London in the chapel at Fulham Palace, and this was done as a gesture of the respect which the Bishop felt for his father's memory. He was ordained without church or title, and he remained in residence at Cambridge for three more years. But he served the Curacy of Barton for six months, and rendered help to various friends in nearby counties from time to time. These were years when Whitefield and the Wesleys were at the height of their struggle with clergy and bishops, years when England was being stirred and shaken by the field preaching of the Oxford evangelists. But Venn's views of spiritual truth were still vague as vague could be, and he had no distinct idea of right or wrong in the realm of theology. The truth was that all his early training, all the influence of family pride and the prejudice of education, were in favour of the doctrines and tenets of the old-fashioned High Churchmen. He had a high idea of true clerical decorum in the style of that school, and he strove hard to base his early ministry on its principles. Thus he taught the poor once a week in his own rooms and gave away tracts at Barton, and he was still remembered with kindly affection by the people there after thirty years. He was still a stranger to the blessings of the Christian Evangel, and his zeal was not the zeal of an enlightened disciple; but he was scrupulous in all that he saw to be his duty, and there sprang up in his heart an intense desire to live to the glory of God. He recalled in September 1785:

> Well I remember when in the midst of great darkness respect-
> ing the Person, the work and office of my adored Redeemer,
> in the midst of utter ignorance of the Law and my own total
> corruption, I felt this desire, strong and urgent, from day-to
> day; and it hath never departed from me, and never will![5]

Supernatural was that desire; it was like the bud which foretells
the fruit and the blossom. It taught him to walk night by night
in the cloisters of Trinity College while the great bell of St.
Mary's was tolling out the hour of nine, so that the alternate
strokes and silence of that grand old bell might give rise
to a train of solemn thought and meditation on the things of
eternity. It made him strict to heed the soft voice of conscience
within, and to act up to all the light which he knew to be his.
Nor was this strong sense of integrity without reward, though
the final test came in a way that modern readers would not
expect. He was extremely fond of cricket, and was one of the
best players Cambridge could field. He played his last game
in a match between Surrey and All England the week before he
was ordained; he helped his side to win, and the stumps were
drawn in triumph. But he walked off the field and tossed his bat
aside with the remark that if anyone wanted it he might have it.
The one reason which he gave was that he would be ordained
on the Sunday, and he would not have it said of him as one in
Orders, 'Well struck, Parson!' Nothing would induce him to
reverse this decision; not the arguments of sport or health, nor
the persuasions of Tutors and Fellows. And who will say that
he was wrong in days when so many clergy loved horse and
hounds far more than they loved the souls of men and women?
He was prompted by a noble idea of duty at a time when men
were often content with mean enough standards of office. Venn
himself in after years used to say that he owed his soul to the
resolute self-denial with which he was able by the Grace of
God to obey the clear voice of conscience in this matter; for
the point on which a crisis turns may be small enough, but the
crisis itself may be fraught with eternal destinies.[6]

But Venn's worldly friends dropped away, and he was left to walk alone. In July 1750 he left Cambridge and took a curacy with the Rector of St. Matthew, Friday Street, in London, and of West Horsley, near Guildford, in Surrey. He was required to spend the summer months in London and the winter months at Horsley, and he carried on his work in line with this routine for the next four years with great profit to his own soul. His deep fidelity to the demands of his office bore fruit of its own kind, and he made a mark on the life of the parish which was not soon effaced. Thirty or forty of his poorer neighbours at Horsley used to attend his household prayers, and the number who knelt at the Lord's Table increased from twelve to sixty. His zeal and activity soon gave offence to the nearby clergy who sneered at him as a Methodist or an Enthusiast, though as yet he knew none of the men who had been labelled with such terms of reproach. But though he still walked like a man in the shadows he was now close to the regions of light and truth. The solitude and seclusion of a country parish gave him time for reading and prayer, and the honest use of such means led him on to further blessing. He read Law's *Serious Call to a Devout and Holy Life* repeatedly and attentively, and he tried to frame his conduct on the pattern which it displayed. He planned the hours of each day so as to combine duty with devotion; he engaged in frequent fasts and lonely walks to build up his soul in the love and communion of God. He made it a habit to ride over the Downs for exercise, and to chant as he rode the noble strains of the *Te Deum*. His whole heart was for God, and God was not far off; his eyes were towards the sunrise, and the sunrise was even then at hand.

He kept a diary of the state of his mind, and found that it taught him lessons of which he was woefully ignorant. 'I began to keep my diary', he recalled in November 1777, 'hoping to find myself in everything exact, and almost without fault; how was I surprised and ashamed when innumerable deficiencies and blots and corruptions appeared!'[7] He tried to pin down the slightest alienation of thought from the love and fear of

God, the slightest rising of irregular passion or desire, and his failure to reach the full height of perfect moral purity grieved him intensely. It forced the old problem into his mind, even when he stood up to preach in the pulpit: 'Why do you impose upon others a standard to which you are conscious you have not yourself attained?'[8] Thus little by little he found out the defects in Law's system of thought and life, and he resolved thenceforth to call no man master; and little by little he found out the message which the gospel intends for the fallen and the sinful, and he perceived therewith that the only hope for such is in the mercy and the merits of the Saviour. He had begun to search the Book of God to hear what God might say, and he found that the root of all true faith is in the blood and righteousness of our Immanuel. 'I am myself a witness what pains a man may take to go to heaven,' he wrote in September 1771, 'and yet be quite in the dark!'[9] But the scales were falling from his eyes, and the tone of his preaching had sensibly altered. It was a change which no one could deny, although it was not yet complete; and it was due to the work of God in his heart, without help from friends or human agents at all. His four years at Horsley drew to an end while he was still pressing towards the light, but they closed round a man who was in a state of mind and soul quite unlike his state less than four years before.

In 1754 he was installed as Curate of Clapham, and for five years he was engaged in an untiring ministry, partly in that pleasant country village and partly in its crowded mother city. These five years at Clapham were the grand turning-point, both in his private history and in his public ministry; they saw him thoroughly established in all the leading doctrines of the New Testament Evangel. He was still quite unknown to the Oxford evangelists, but it would seem that he had been one of Wesley's occasional hearers. On March 21, 1754 he wrote to tell him that his words had often been 'as thunder to his drowsy soul', and to beg him for a charge with regard to the flock of which he had now been made the shepherd. 'It is the request', he wrote, 'of one who though he differs from you, and possibly ever may in some points, yet must acknowledge the benefit and light he has received from your works and preaching.'[10] He soon proved that he was one of the most active clergy in the church of his day, for he held three Lectureships in London as well as his curacy at Clapham. His regular Sunday duties involved a service at Clapham in the morning, a sermon at St. Alban's, Wood Street, after lunch, and a lecture at St. Swithin's, London-Stone, in the evening. He preached at St. Swithin's again on Tuesday morning, and in his father's old church at St. Antholin's on Wednesday morning. He preached at Clapham again on Thursday evening, and there were often other engagements as well. Thus he had at least six sermons to preach each week, and he was soon obliged to preach only from notes; no man could write six fresh sermons a week, and it was sheer necessity which taught him the art of extempore preaching. He was in fact the first London preacher to break through the custom of reading his sermons, and to revive the old way of a free address to the conscience; he was even before William Romaine in this respect, though this was the time when Romaine first began to attract the notice of churchmen.[11]

There had been no one of like mind with Venn at Horsley, but that was quite altered at Clapham. His duties in London brought him into contact with the Rev. Thomas Broughton, who had been one of the original band of Methodists at Oxford;[12] and his work at Clapham led to a warm friendship with the Rev. Thomas Haweis, who had been one of the converts of Walker of Truro.[13] Above all, it was at Clapham that his intimate fellowship was born with John Thornton, the young banker whose piety was already full of promise for the future. Venn came to love him, and the two men were soon one in their faith in Christ. 'Oh that God would make me in my sphere,' he wrote in April 1769, 'such a tree of righteousness as he is!'[14] In his house he soon met many of the leading figures in the spiritual movement of the 'fifties, and they helped him to yet clearer views of truth. Thus in 1755 he met Whitefield, who preached in his church at Clapham; it was a momentous day for Venn, and he never ceased to feel the magnetic hold of the mighty preacher on his soul. Whitefield often went to Thornton's home to expound the Word of Life to a crowded audience, and Venn was never absent from such an assembly.[15] Then there were two other circumstances which helped to educate his soul and to clarify his views. The first was a severe illness in 1756, when he was forced to lay down his work for some nine months; it was a long break in his normal round of ceaseless activity, and it gave him time for reflection and self-examination. The other was his marriage in 1757 to the daughter of a well-known divine, for in her he found a helpmate whose whole faith was truly congenial to his own soul. He had begun to meet opposition from men who could not brook moral restraint in the gospel and who wished for no more than a formal system in their worship, but this only strengthened his grasp of truth and cleared his views of Christ. It was observed that his preaching and his conversation took on a more elevated spirit, for he had now struggled through the mists of doubt and self-denial into noon-day light and sunshine.

But there was yet one more experience which was used of God to perfect the work of grace, and this was his introduction to that group of eminent Christian men and women who had gathered round the Countess of Huntingdon. It was no doubt through George Whitefield that he first met this noble Mother in Israel, and she seems to have been the means under God of advice to which he owed the full joy of salvation. In the autumn months of 1757 she persuaded him to join George Whitefield on a preaching campaign in the west of England; but she soon felt dissatisfied, in a measure at least, with his presentation of the gospel message. 'O my friend,' she wrote, 'we can make no atonement to a violated law; we have no inward holiness of our own; the Lord Jesus Christ is the Lord our Righteousness!'[16] This frank letter seems to have made him give fresh thought to the ground of his standing before God, and further interaction with Whitefield seems to have taught him the secret of a solid peace and satisfaction through the blood and righteousness of Christ our Saviour. It was in the self-same year that Whitefield wrote to Lady Huntingdon in the highest testimony to Venn's spiritual maturity:

> The worthy Venn is valiant for the truth, a son of thunder. He labours abundantly, and his ministry has been owned of the Lord in the conversion of sinners. Thanks be to God for such an instrument as this to strengthen our hands.... Your exertions in bringing him to a clearer knowledge of the everlasting gospel have indeed been blessed. He owes Your Ladyship much under God, and I believe his whole soul is gratitude to the Divine Author of mercies, and to you, the honoured instrument in leading him to the fountain of truth.[17]

This is a most significant letter, and its testimony is unexceptional; Whitefield's judgment was based on the widest experience, and he was not the man to be easily satisfied in the case of a soul.

It was in the course of this tour that Venn and Whitefield came to Cheltenham, where the door of the church was slammed shut in their face. Whitefield promptly preached from a tomb in the churchyard, and Venn described the scene in a letter to Lady Huntingdon: 'O with what eloquence, what energy, what melting tenderness, did Mr Whitefield beseech sinners to be reconciled to God!'[18] The crowd seemed as though chained to the ground as the great preacher came to an end; but then Venn and others were surrounded by souls broken under a sense of guilt and famished for the Bread of Life. It was a grand experience for Venn, and he never forgot the things his eyes had seen. Walker of Truro went to visit him a few months later, and described him as 'a London clergyman...now brought to believe for himself... a man very desirable in his temper, humble and teachable'.[19] Thus he soon came to be recognized as a true fellow-workman in that noble band of evangelists of whom Whitefield was the chief and captain, and his marked gifts as a preacher soon won him a leading place in their ranks. In 1758 Lady Huntingdon held a 'spiritual rout' twice a week in her London home at which Venn often preached to a fashionable congregation of Lords and Ladies;'[20] in 1759 she arranged a series of meetings for prayer in her private quarters owing to the threat of a French invasion, and Venn joined with Whitefield and the Wesleys in the ministry to the aristocrats who were assembled for these occasions.[21] His deep veneration for this gracious Lady grew with the years, and a passing remark in one of his letters from Bath, in November 1769, gives us a clue to his profound regard for her: 'In Lady Huntingdon, I see a star of the first magnitude.... How do works, the works of faith and love, speak and preach Jesus Christ in that devoted servant of His!'[22]

In 1759 the Benefice of Huddersfield fell vacant in Yorkshire, and the Earl of Dartmouth secured its offer for the Curate of Clapham. Venn's wife did not relish the thought of a change from the warmth of Surrey to the bleak hills and dales of far-off Yorkshire; and he knew that it would be much to his loss in point of income in view of his growing expense with small children. Some weeks passed by before he could make up his mind; then he resolved to ride north and make his choice on the spot. Huddersfield is now the seat of a large city population which is absorbed in the toils of many manufactures; but in Venn's time it was still classed by the *Gazette* as a village of West Riding. The full parish embraced a large country district with its various outlying hamlets, but the total population did not amount to more than five thousand.[23] Thus it is not correct to say that Venn was called to a dark and crowded city, and it is a mistake to think that he was faced with the huge and cumbrous masses of a modern township; but the parish itself was dark enough and wild enough in all conscience, a parish whose people were ignorant of truth and immoral in life. Two years before, in May 1757, Wesley had ridden over the mountains from Manchester to Huddersfield, and his impressions were by no means uplifting:

> A wilder people I never saw in England, the men, women and children filled the street as we rode along, and appeared just ready to devour us. They were however tolerably quiet while I preached; only a few pieces of dirt were thrown, and the bell-man came in the middle of the sermon. I had almost done when they began to ring the bells.'[24]

No one was more able to judge and less prone to exaggerate than John Wesley; he knew the Three Kingdoms as no other man of his age knew them, and he had seen all sides of life in city and country as few others ever see them. But he was still of the same mind on his return two years later, just at the time when Venn had to weigh up the call: 'July 23rd 1759,' he wrote, 'I preached near Huddersfield to the wildest congregation I have seen in Yorkshire.'[25]

Wesley's remarks are borne out by one of Venn's old hearers who was to say in late old age: 'Mr Venn was a very bold man; he was afraid of no one. If he had not been of that sort, he ought never to have come here, for he came into a den of lions and tigers.'[26] There was little enough in the outward aspect to attract Venn's favour, but the long ride north on horseback had helped to fix his mind. He viewed the parish, and saw the finger of God; he met the people, and felt the challenge of souls. He wrote home to his wife:

> I am now fully determined that it is the will of God we should come here, I have gone through much perplexity and uneasy suspense; being one day in this mind through some favourable circumstance, another day in quite a different opinion. I made earnest prayer to our most loving and gracious Father that He would look down upon His poor doubting child, unwilling to take a step which there might be cause to repent of, and fearful of doing wrong, either by removing or by refusing the situation. I have since enjoyed an ease of mind and satisfaction in the prospect of settling at Huddersfield, quite undisturbed.[27]

He preached there on several occasions, and one of the tradesmen who was won for Christ seemed like a seal on his call. 'I well remember his first coming to Huddersfield, and the first sermon he preached,' an old hearer recalled long years after. 'It was on that text, My heart's desire for Israel is that they may be saved; and it was as true of himself as of St. Paul.'[28] He was full of joy and eager anticipation as he wrote once more to his wife and told her all his heart: 'But what is best of all, such a vast multitude of souls to hear—under my care, fourteen hundred families! And out of other parishes, together my audience this afternoon could not be less than upwards of three thousand!'[29]

Thus Venn became Vicar of Huddersfield at the age of thirty-five, and for twelve years made full proof of his ministry. These were the prime years of his life, and Huddersfield proved to be the grand scene of his labours in the gospel. He went there with a small purse, but with a brave heart; he had neither rank nor fortune to back his name, but he had the love of Christ in his heart and the Word of Truth on his tongue. His whole soul was now fixed in its apprehension of the leading doctrines of the gospel, and he took up his new duties in the full vigour of mind and body, and the full exercise of all his faculties. He had none of the technique or machinery of a modern parish, and was therefore confined to the use of one great method; he was forced to be a man of one thing, like a soldier of one weapon, and to devote himself to the great work of a preacher. It was his lot to prove that a faithful preacher could turn the world of weavers and farmers in their Yorkshire dales as upside down as did the preaching of the Evangelists in the case of the peasants and craftsmen of Judaea and Galilee. He soon drew such overflowing congregations that large numbers who came could not secure a seat at all, and great power fell upon those who sat at his feet. He took pains to make the service bright and real, and he was never afraid to try simple innovations. Thus a short and solemn exhortation would precede the service to remind his hearers that they stood in the presence and beneath the eye of the God of Heaven; and a brief and earnest explanation would follow in due course to drive home the meaning of the Psalms and Lessons. His sermons were never read, but were preached from notes in a way that gave full play to the tenderness and compassion with which his heart overflowed. But his stated work on Sundays was not a tenth of his labours throughout the week, and much of his time was spent on horseback as he rode to distant corners of his sprawling parish. He would hunt out obscure parishioners who dwelt in tiny homes and lonely farms, and would preach as often as ten times a week to many who would not come to church.[30]

Such a workman was not to go without a rich reward; the seed sown with such singular earnestness soon bore fruit of a glorious character. 'You know', he wrote, 'I was merely a voice which said, Behold the Lamb of God!'[31] a cottage room or the open air were always as welcome to him as a desk or pulpit, and the impact of such a man on his parish was powerful and permanent. He knew how to move multitudes to tears and repentance, and great numbers were seized with deep concern for their sins and their souls. People flocked in from the distant hamlets with just one question on their lips, and that was the jailer's question of old as to what they should do to be saved. His own daughter recalled in her old age the kind of thing that would happen three or four times in the morning.

> I used to hear Ruth come running across the long passage; the door would open, and she would say, a man wants to speak to you about his soul! Tell him to come in, my father would say. I remember the look of many of them to this day, with channels upon their black cheeks where the tears were running. Oh Sir, they would begin at once to say with eagerness, I have never slept since last Thursday night! Oh Sir! your sermon![32]

Hearers came from far beyond the parish proper, and they came again and again. Two close friends who once came from Leeds, fifteen miles away, were so moved with all that they had heard that not one word broke the silence on their way home until they were within a mile of Leeds. Such then was the preacher who used to beg his friends to help him on their knees so that he might speak with a voice like the roar of thunder till the evil of sin was owned, and then that he might pour the balm of the gospel into the wounds of the spirit.[33] Few parish ministers in English history have so moved and shaken town and county by the simple art of preaching; Richard Baxter in his work at

Kidderminster seems to be the truest fellow of Henry Venn in his years at Huddersfield.

Meanwhile he had made his testimony known and felt in many parts of England by means of his pen, for it was in 1763 that he published *The Complete Duty of Man*. This book was meant as an answer to a book which had first appeared more than a century before, in 1657, under the title of *The Whole Duty of Man*. The author's name was never known, but this earlier work had leapt at once into fame and semi-official recognition. It was published only three years prior to the Restoration, and it soon swept into vogue at the height of popular reaction from Puritan Theology. It was hailed as a clear statement of sound and sober Church teaching, and was given a place of its own with unique prestige in the life of the Church. It was made the basis for instruction in the Charity Schools, and it was chained in many churches like the Cranmer Bible for the common people to come and read. *The Whole Duty of Man* was a book which tried to reduce all the tenets of a saving faith to the most prosaic elements, and it seemed to make eternal life a thing of doing and duty. It was a book which helped to bring men up in the school of morals that taught Nelson the code of his great Trafalgar signal; but it had no message that could furrow with long gutters of tears the cheeks of men like the Kingswood miners or the Yorkshire farmers. That was why the Evangelicals of the eighteenth century were so bent on pointing out its defects; Whitefield for one brought great obloquy on himself for saying that its author knew as little of the gospel as did Mohammed. But Venn did a better thing than merely join in oral reproach; he set out to give the world an adequate substitute. Not one of his brethren had more right than he had to look on this as his particular province, to provide new converts with a clear and solid system of doctrinal and practical Christianity; he had met most of the average Christian's difficulties in life, and he knew where to look for Divine succour and for consolation in trial.

Venn first took the book in hand while he was still at Clapham, but it was not finished until he had settled into his stride at Huddersfield. 'My book advances but slowly,' he wrote in June 1760, 'and I must in earnest so apply that it may be finished by the beginning of next year.'[34] 'If it were not for…encouraging approbation, I should faint in my book,' he wrote six months later; 'but this, when I receive it, is a strong incentive to persevere.'[35] It came out at last in 1763, and was hailed at once as one of the most popular manuals for the soul which had yet appeared. It ran through some twenty editions in its first fifty years, and news of its value came in from all quarters, from the New World no less than from the Old. It dealt with the ethics of man's daily life in detail, just as did *The Whole Duty of Man*; but there was a radical difference in the spirit of its approach to the same old problems. Venn laid it down in his Preface that Christ the Law-Giver will speak in vain until Christ the Sin-Bearer is truly known.[36] 'The sacred consonance…of his own life', Sir James Stephen affirms, '…rendered his conceptions of duty eminently pure, large, and consistent…and imparted a rich and cordial unction to his persuasions to obedience.'[37] He wrote in the stately and rather high-flown style which was then the standard of literary excellence, and the book had a wide circulation in the reading classes of its own age. But the modern reader feels that this old style is 'neither Saxon, nor sparkling, nor racy, nor pithy, nor anecdotal, nor pictorial,'[38] and there are few as a result who would read it today. The fashion of warfare has changed, and old weapons are laid aside; but that must not blind us to the fact that Venn had forged a sword which made the warriors of those days strong for the field.

Venn has left no journal of his movements, and we cannot trace his footsteps as we can those of Wesley or Whitefield; but a close examination of *The Life and Times of Lady Huntingdon* shows that he preached year by year in many pulpits beside his own. It is clear that he made various excursions through the English counties, and did as much as an itinerant Evangelist as parish duties would permit. He was on the closest terms of friendship with the leading Evangelicals of the day, and we can hardly doubt that the half of his labours outside his own parish are still untold. Wesley and Whitefield, Grimshaw and Romaine, were no strangers in his home and pulpit, and we can well believe that he helped them as much as he could in return. In all vital points of spiritual truth and conduct, in creed and in practice, in his judgment of what the times required, he was one with such men. Therefore he stood in the breach at their side, and did all that lay in his power to strengthen their hands in God. In November 1759 he travelled with Lady Huntingdon from Brighton to Everton where John Berridge was in the midst of revival; on three successive days he preached indoors and outdoors to enormous crowds which grew to some ten thousand.[39] In August 1761 Newton tells us how Venn surprised him with a brief visit. 'It pleased God to give me influence to get him St. George's pulpit' in Liverpool, he wrote, 'and I had the pleasure to hear him there proclaim the truth in a bold, lively, engaging, and powerful discourse.'[40] Later in the same year he took part with Romaine and Berridge at the opening of Lady Huntingdon's chapel at Brighton; Venn took charge for a time, and one of his converts while preaching at Oathall was an old man who had had his hundredth birthday.[41] Then in 1762 he joined Lady Huntingdon with Romaine and Whitefield to attend Wesley's Annual Conference at Leeds.[42] In 1763 he was preaching in London three times a Sunday in July, and then he accompanied Lady Huntingdon on a visit to Tunbridge Wells.[43] In 1765 he took part with Romaine and Whitefield at the opening of the Chapel at Bath; it was in this Chapel that the bishops were wont to be smuggled into curtained seats where they could hear and yet remain unseen![44]

In the course of 1766 he went down to Brighton again, where he was fired and encouraged by Fletcher's example; then he went on to Bath, where he rejoiced in Romaine's gracious ministry. He passed on to Bristol en route for Trevecca, where he spent three days with Howel Harris. 'In a long tour I have been taking I have seen some glorious instances of the power of the Lord Jesus,' he told Newton; 'Mr Howel Harris has a large company of people—I think the most excellent I ever saw.'[45] He moved on to become a guest with Riland and Conyers in the Shropshire home of Thomas Powley, and all that he had seen and heard made him cry out in prayer and praise: 'Ride on, Thou Most Mighty, according to Thy worship and renown!'[46] In June 1767 Lady Huntingdon was for some days a guest in Venn's Huddersfield Vicarage, and in July she made Kippax for some weeks the centre of a remarkable evangelistic enterprise; Venn, and Fletcher, and Whitefield, and others, toured the county, preaching to vast crowds and begging them to flee from the wrath to come.[47] In 1768 Lady Huntingdon took possession of Trevecca on lease as a college to train converted men for the ministry, and Venn was linked with Romaine and Fletcher in the initial plans. In March 1769, at John Thornton's request as High Sheriff for his county, he preached the Assize Sermon at Kingston, and then in the next eight weeks he preached some twenty sermons, with Romaine and Whitefield as his fellow-workers, in Lady Huntingdon's London mansion.[48] 'What has most pleased me', he wrote, 'is to find how many spiritual children of whom I knew nothing the Lord has given me in this city.'[49] In October 1769 he set out to preach for a few Sundays in the chapel at Bath, and one of his letters traces out his journey through Sheffield and Chatsworth, Northampton and St. Albans, Reading and Pewsey. 'On Sunday evening last', he wrote from Bath, 'there was such a crowded audience…as there never was before. The chapel doors were set open, and people stood in the court as far as the houses.'[50] It was a most crowded season, and great numbers of the nobility were induced to attend Venn's preaching; the Hon. and Rev. Walter Shirley and the Earl of Buchan were among his converts, and we cannot tell how many of their fellows he was able to lead into the way of peace. Very choice was the band of friends whose hearts were linked with Venn in love for a common Master; friends like Whitefield and Grimshaw, Wesley and Fletcher, Berridge and Romaine, and a score of others whose praise is known to all. A few hours' ride to the north was William Grimshaw, whose apostolic ministry at Haworth was near its end; Venn rode over to be with him on his death-bed in 1763, and preached his funeral sermon to an overflowing congregation in the Luddenden burial ground and in the church at Haworth. Many years later, in 1779, he recalled him in a letter to his son, and ranked him with his 'very dear friends, now high in glory'.[51] Away to the west was Fletcher of Madeley, who was almost as dear to Venn as to Wesley. 'A genius, and a man of fire,' Venn would call him, 'all on the stretch to do good, to lose not a day, not an hour!'[52] In 1776 Venn met him at St. Neots and became so absorbed in the conversation that Fletcher had to remind him playfully of the meal still on the table.[53] In 1777 he spent six weeks beneath the same roof with Fletcher at Bath, and said of him: 'Sir, Mr Fletcher was a luminary. A luminary, did I say? He was a sun. I have known all the great men for these fifty years, but I have known none like him.'[54] After his death in 1785 he summed up his salient qualities in one typical incident:

> His humility was so unfeigned and so deep that when I thanked him for two sermons he had one day preached to my people at Huddersfield, he answered as no man ever did to me; with eyes and hands uplifted, he exclaimed, Pardon, pardon, pardon, O my God! It went to my very soul; I shall never forget it.[55]

Venn's warm regard for John Wesley was not disturbed by time or by controversy, and the proof of Wesley's friendship was made clear in his plans for the Huddersfield Methodists. Wesley's preachers had set up a society at great hazard before Venn came to the parish, and they wanted to carry on as auxiliaries to his teaching. But Venn felt that this would not be in the best interests of his own ministry, and a tender point thus emerged. Venn and Wesley talked it over at Bradford in 1761, and they agreed that the preachers should not come more than once a month.[56] Then in 1764 Wesley went still further to please Venn, and agreed that their visits should be entirely suspended for the space of a year.[57] Wesley's tokens of true goodwill were sealed by his sermons from Venn's pulpit, and by the last mention of Venn in his journal: 'Dec. 3rd 1776; I crossed over to St. Neots, and had an hour's friendly conversation with Mr Venn.'[58]

Away down in London there was William Romaine, and Venn joined him many a time in his ministry at Lady Huntingdon's chapels. 'My old friend and fellow labourer', he wrote of him in April 1783, 'and a wonder of a man, who seems now drawing towards the end of his highly-honoured labours.'[59] There was quaint John Berridge, his close neighbour in later years. 'He is a blessed man,' Venn wrote in November 1771, 'and a true Calvinist!'[60] Time only confirmed his judgment, and in December 1782 he wrote again: 'Just such a Calvinist as he is, I wish all ministers of Christ to be.'[61] There was bluff John Newton, who used to ride over to Huddersfield from Liverpool before he was ordained as Curate of Olney. Thus in April 1763 Newton records such a visit: 'A hearty reception from Mr Venn at Huddersfield; heard him twice on Sunday.... In every exercise, in the whole of his converse and carriage, he seems eminent and exemplary.'[62] Thus too in November 1776 Venn wrote to him: 'I never long forget either of you, my dear friends; I have much communion with you, and remember you where I can do you the most good.'[63] Newton was a welcome guest in Venn's home as long as life and health allowed. 'He is my brother', we hear Venn exclaim, 'and fellow servant to our adorable Lord !'[64] But of all the friends who learned to love him, there was none more welcome to Venn's own heart than George Whitefield. 'I think', says Ryle, 'his unhesitating attachment to Whitefield to the very last a singularly noble trait in his character.'[65] In March 1763 Venn wrote with glee: 'Mr Whitefield is here on his way to Scotland!'[66] Venn never failed to join him in Yorkshire, preaching in church or cottage, in street or meadow.[67] In October 1767 Whitefield spent two or three days at Huddersfield Vicarage at a time when Venn was in great distress through the death of his wife; it was his last visit to the north of England, and the last sermons he preached in Yorkshire were preached from Venn's pulpit.[68] But the first three months of 1769 found Venn with Whitefield and Romaine and the Wesleys, constantly assembled in Lady Huntingdon's

London home for preaching and Christian fellowship. Their last meeting was marked by sermons from Venn and Whitefield, and all sang the Doxology. In September 1769 Whitefield set sail for the New World, and in September 1770 he died at Newbury Port. On November 18 Wesley preached a memorial sermon for his friend in London, and on the same day Venn poured out his soul in a noble sermon at Bath.

Venn's twelve years at Huddersfield saw a marvellous change in the life of the parish; he turned the world upside down, and the church inside out. 'They call us mad,' he wrote, 'but God distinguishes all the world of unawakened sinners by that very appellation. Madness, He says, is in their heart.'[69] Thus he used the mighty lever of the gospel message to move the hearts of the cold and careless, and his powerful ministry shook both town and country with the power of heaven. No just idea of his pulpit gifts can be formed from the handful of those sermons which are preserved in print, but that he was a great preacher is clear from the profound regard in which he was held by Lady Huntingdon and other distinguished Evangelicals. His great popularity, even with Whitefield's most ardent hearers, and the unmistakable results of his preaching speak for themselves. Ryle's shrewd surmise that his sermons were of the kind which are good to hear but hard to read would explain why the defects in his printed sermons did not impress themselves on his auditors at the time when they were delivered.[70] It was his fond custom to write at the head of all his sermon notes the caption in Greek:

Δόξα τῷ θεῷμοὶ   ἁμαρτωλῷ ἔλεος
GLORY TO GOD!   MERCY TO ME A SINNER!

He carried this spirit from the study to the pulpit, and his own words in a letter to a friend in 1766 let us see what this meant. 'When I come into the pulpit', he wrote, 'it is after study, prayers, and cries for the people; I speak as plainly, and enter into all the cases of the congregation as minutely as I am able.'[71] He preached from notes, and no shorthand record of their content remains; and no printed sermon could give a true idea of his forceful action or his animated delivery. Face and voice, eyes and arms, his whole manner in the pulpit took his hearers by storm and clothed his words with tremendous solemnity. He looked so stern that men trembled when he dealt with the Law and its thunders, but his face lit up with a smile and his eyes filled with tears when he turned to Grace and its offers.

Such a preacher was soon a power for God all through the West Riding of Yorkshire, and such a ministry was bound to leave deep and lasting benefit in its train. He spoke from a full mind, and therefore with singular aptitude; he spoke from a full heart, and therefore with tenderest sympathy. His profound sense of responsibility gave an artless force to his pleas that few could resist; his immense store of mature experience gave an endless charm to his words that none could exhaust. In 1824, more than fifty years after he had left the parish, his grandson paid a visit to the scene of his labours. He went to find out how far the recollection of those labours might have survived the lapse of half a century, and he found that there were surprising examples of his success which still remained. He was able to see all who had once known Venn and who still lived in the parish, all who had owed their souls to him and who still tried to walk with God. They were all in the middle or lower ranks of life, and he compiled a deeply interesting collection of memorials. One man recalled the vast crowd which filled the church the first time he heard Venn preach; all were silent, and many were weeping. People used to come in scores from Longwood, three miles away; they would stop at Fir's End on the way home, and talk long and earnestly over what they had heard. To them it was the House of God, and the Gate of Heaven. 'He was such a preacher as I never heard before nor since,' said one old man; 'he struck upon the passions like no other man.'[72] One old woman spoke of him with great emotion and deep reverence; things he had said still pierced her mind and wrung her soul. An old man of nearly eighty said that nothing could have kept him away when Venn was the preacher. 'I have often wept at his sermons,' he said; 'I could have stood to hear him till morning.'[73] Young Venn felt that Huddersfield as he found it was like the prophet's olive tree after the harvest was over; there remained only two or three berries on the top of the uppermost bough. But if such bright tokens and such clear proofs of the power of Henry Venn's ministry could still be found after the long lapse of fifty years; what are we to suppose was the effect of his preaching in his own day and to his own generation?

Venn was a man of middle height and impressive bearing. His face was round and ruddy in complexion, full of good humour and pleasantness; his voice was strong and striking in resonance, full of great kindness and affection. He was as true in generous sympathies as he was rich in liberal charities, and he kept an open house and a warm welcome for his friends and fellow servants in the gospel. Thornton and the Earl of Dartsmouth helped to swell his income by their gifts, and his style of living was simple but genteel.[74] But his labours were not without their cost, for they imposed a very severe tax on both mind and body. His heart was drawn out in ceaseless yearning for his flock, and he was never satisfied with what he had done. He was ever riding here and preaching there, for there were cottage meetings on weekdays as well as public worship on Sundays. He did all that lay in his power to make Sunday a holy day, and to make the Church services real and reverent. He took great pains in teaching the children, and drew up a detailed explanation of the Church catechism for their use. But the result of such excessive exertion was that he reached a point which proved ruinous both to health and usefulness. He had written in 1762:

> It is a hard matter to keep the exact medium, to be. . . very zealous for our God, and not exert ourselves beyond what the mortal body can bear; it is certainly the better extreme... to spend and be spent, even to the shortening a little a short life at best in such a manner as to refute lukewarmness by example, than to live a longer life in a manner not so visibly contrary to it.[75]

He went to the better extreme with all his might, but not without warning as he drew closer to the edge. In February 1766 a chest complaint increased so much that for seven months he could do next to nothing; he could only speak once a week, and not even then without suffering for it.[76] But the chief cause of his final breakdown was the sudden death of his wife in September 1767. 'Jesus!' he cried, 'hold me by Thy right hand till I reach the same blessed haven!'[77]

He had not been without burdens prior to this, but this was by far the sorest loss he had yet sustained. Other trials he could bear with a light heart while his wife stood by him; her good sense and prudence, her warm love and insight, had been his strength and stay. But her death placed such a load of care and anxiety on his shoulders that his health failed outright a year or two later. He was left in sole charge of his five small children, and the care of a home without the help of a wife or mother is a burden that few can bear. It soon became clear that he would die at his post unless he could secure a long and complete rest from all duty; his chest complaint had grown steadily worse, and in 1770 he was forced to seek a real change at Bath. It was here that his friend, Lord Chief Baron Smythe, a Commissioner of the Great Seal, offered him a Living in the Chancellor's gift at Yelling. His own parishioners pleaded with him to stay, and he was loath enough to leave. 'Were I to consult my own ease and peace,' he wrote, 'I should never stir from Huddersfield.'[78] Had they urged their case with less vehemence and more tenderness, he could not have found it in his heart to refuse. But his cough was severe, and there were other and worse signs of consumption; he could only preach once in a fortnight, and the effort left him prostrate for several days. He was only 47 years of age, but he was much older than the tally of his years; he saw that he could serve them no longer, and that he would only die in harness if he were to return. But life might be prolonged if he moved to a new and quiet sphere of service, and the call to Yelling came at a time which showed the hand of God in a way he could not mistake. Thus his mind was made up, to the great sorrow of Huddersfield, and his last two or three months there were the most affecting of all; the church was packed from an early hour if he were to preach, and vast numbers were forced away for want of room. His last sermon was preached on Easter Day, March 30, 1771, and the whole parish was deeply moved; he could hardly speak for emotion, nor the congregation hear for affection. A twelve-year ministry of rare grace and power had reached its close, and his heart was more than full as he faced his flock for the last time. 'No human being', he told Lady Huntingdon, 'can tell how keenly I feel this separation from a people I have dearly loved.'[79]

'I go to Yelling as a dying man'; so Venn had written in November 1770:[80] But the rest and the change saved his life, and his constitution rallied until he could do his work with comparative ease; he came to die, but lived on for twenty-six years. The Church of The Holy Cross in Yelling served a small agricultural parish on the south-east border of Huntingdon, twelve miles to the west of Cambridge. It would be difficult to think of a greater contrast than that between Yelling and the parish he had left in Yorkshire, and he felt it very keenly. He found that it was a region 'very thinly sown with people;' there were not more than 160 souls all told.[81] His new congregation was composed of country yokels, a few dull, cold, impassive labourers, who had no clear vision of truth at all, and he could not even dismiss the old curate without risk of a breach all round.[82] 'What a change, from thousands to a company of one hundred, from a people generally enlightened and many converted to one yet sitting in darkness and ignorant of the first principles of the gospel!' So he wrote in August 1771; 'a change painful indeed, yet unavoidable; with a heavy heart therefore did I yesterday begin to address my new hearers.'[83] But he preached morning and evening, and never to a more attentive audience; and in the evening to four times the number that had ever been in the church before. It was not long before he saw the fruit of his desire; those ploughmen and shepherds awoke to new life at the sound of his preaching. 'Here I begin to see all that I saw at Huddersfield,' he wrote within the next few weeks;

'amazement, attention, conviction, tears, and a vast increase of hearers for a country so desert as this, where a hundred is more than a thousand in your place of habitation.[84] Twelve months later the church was full; it was the talk of the country, a thing unknown before. 'I speak not to more than two hundred, sometimes three hundred,' he wrote; 'there are many of them at the distance of eight or ten miles.'[85] His days of usefulness had been renewed, and it gave a new lease of life to his health as well as his work. 'On Sundays', he exclaimed, 'I am still enabled to speak six hours at three different times to my own great surprise. O the goodness of God in raising me up!'[86] The true value of his preaching was soon discovered in spite of his seclusion, and he had the joy of seeing God's seal on his labours even as in Yorkshire.

But, on the whole, life at Yelling was quiet and uneventful, 'a life of apostolic simplicity.'[87] His second marriage in 1771 did much to restore his happiness, and his home life was a model of peaceful bliss. He rose at five in the morning and spent the day in a round of sacred duty. Nine months had to elapse before a single soul came of his own accord to speak of spiritual need, but his patience had its reward and his house was at last thronged with daily callers. Twenty or more would crowd into his room to share in the household worship, and they drank with him from the wells of life. It was seldom that he figured in the public eye as he had done in Yorkshire, but he still found many outlets for his loving witness. It was only a nine-mile ride to Everton Vicarage and good old John Berridge, and they often met as twin souls to cheer and strengthen each other. Venn had never felt bound by strict scruples for church order, and his old friend Berridge had no difficulty in getting him to preach in barns up and down the country.[88] In December 1773 he was preaching at Bath,[89] and in 1775 we find him in Reading and in Kidderminster.[90] In August 1776 he was preaching for his former curate, Riland, in Birmingham,[91] and in 1777 we find him in London and Bath.[92] In 1780 he was attacked by a fever which hung on for nine months; then he set out to try what horseback and Yorkshire could do to mend his health. He was away for nine weeks, and was greatly heartened by his visit to Huddersfield. He drew up as soon as he caught sight of the old steeple three miles away, for he could not refrain from tears. The church was more than filled for the morning service, and in the afternoon hundreds were turned away for want of room. Thirty times in all did he preach in those nine weeks and yet suffered no harm. 'Oh that my health restored and life prolonged,' he cried, 'may be more useful than ever!'[93] In 1782 Rowland Hill opened his Surrey Chapel in London, and Venn preached there as one of his stated supplies each midsummer until his last visit in June 1790.[94] In 1782 he preached to vast numbers in Birmingham,[95] and in the year following he toured the County of Warwickshire.[96] In 1784 we read of a visit to Creaton, where he preached to as many as the church would hold,[97] and in 1785 we hear of his affairs in Yelling where the hearers kept up in zeal and in numbers.[98] Thus it pleased God to crown him with loving-kindness and with tender mercies, and he rejoiced with all his heart to find that grace was with him still.

Yelling was no more than twelve miles across the fields from the Backs of Cambridge, and Venn soon found a new avenue for his ministry with a band of students. In May 1772 he first saw the prospect for such a ministry, and he wrote of the first visit to his Alma Mater which he was then about to make: 'I hope it may please God I may be of some service to the students; I go for no other purpose!'[99] This gave him a contact which soon led to something larger, and a few months later he wrote again: 'There are some excellent young men at College who come to me from the University, as I was in hopes they would.'[100] A number of students who were destined to rank among the most diligent and eminent ministers of the coming generation soon began to come to him for the comfort and counsel of his friendship. We need hardly wonder that they were glad to walk or ride across the fields to see him at Yelling, for they found in him an elder friend who combined the most wholesome and attractive qualities of human nature with the ripe wisdom and sympathy of mature manhood. He was the most delightful companion, and his unfailing happiness cast a spell over his friends. He had a rich flow of conversation which was always sure to please and edify, and his store of anecdotes lent the charm of interest as well as of usefulness to his company.[101] His clear mental vigour and his powers of conversation were such that men would hang on his lips in silence and feast on his words with avidity. Men like Henry Jowett and William Farish owed more than words could tell to Venn; Thomas Robinson of Leicester, and Thomas Thomason of Magdalene College, learned from him much of the wisdom that made them great. There were others like Joseph Jowett and Henry Coulthurst, John Flavel and Charles Jerram. But chief among all Venn's Cambridge friends as life moved towards evening was Charles Simeon. It was in June 1782 that Simeon first met John Venn, whose *Diary* records the fact with laconic brevity: 'June 1st; Commenced acquaintance with Simeon of Kings.'[102] Some weeks later he rode over to meet that 'man of no ordinary character', John Venn's 'dear and honoured father'.[103] 'July 16th,' John Venn records, 'Mr Simeon came at eight, and staid till half past eight at night.[104]

That first visit and the long calm summer day which he spent with Venn paved the way for many further visits, and a friendship of more than usual warmth and fullness sprang up between the young man of twenty-two and one of eight-and-fifty. Venn stood by him all through the first ten years of trial, years that were as critical and as difficult as we can well imagine. He cheered and helped him with warnings and corrections, advice and confidence, at each fresh turn in the struggle with town and gown. 'He comes over to advise with me on every occasion,' wrote Venn in February 1783; 'but the Wonderful Counsellor is with him.'[105] One good result was that Venn's name became better known in Cambridge circles, and more students sought him out with Simeon's introduction. 'There are near twenty promising young students,' he wrote in January 1784; 'several of them come over at times to me.'[106] To visit Venn became a kind of law for all the more earnest men at Cambridge, and no visitors were ever more welcome at the Rectory. 'I have more young students', he wrote in May 1785, 'who visit me from Cambridge, and seem to be going on well.'[107] Twice in 1786, within the first three months, he told Rowland Hill that he had exchanged pulpits with Simeon, and had rejoiced to see certain gownsmen in the congregation. 'I have now been twice at Cambridge,' he wrote, 'and both times have had my heart much warmed with what I have seen and heard.'[108] In 1788 he advised Simeon to do as he had done, and to work right through the main texts of the Bible; this was in response to repeated inquiries for a text, and was the seed thought for Simeon's Skeletons![109] In January 1790 Simeon walked over to Yelling, and slept the night there. 'Oh! How refreshing were his prayers!' cried Venn; 'how profitable his conversation!'[110] In August he went over again, and his presence did the old man's heart good. 'He calls me his father,' wrote Venn; 'he pours out his prayer for me as an instrument from whose counsel he has profited.'[111] Simeon for his part felt that he could never repay his debt of love and gratitude; he was averse to the language of panegyric, but he thought Venn's character beyond all praise. In a letter to John Venn, soon after his death, he summed up his feelings in words that glow with love: 'How great a blessing his conversation and example have been to me will never be known till the Day of Judgment!'[112]

Perhaps his great charm in conversation and his popularity as a preacher may still be judged in some measure by the tone of his letters. Many hundreds of these have been preserved, reaching from youth to old age, and breathing throughout the same spirit of deep and holy rapture or wise and timely advice. Much of his time in the quiet of Yelling was occupied with wide and varied correspondence on themes of spiritual life and experience. 'I reckon I have not written less than seventy letters during the last six months,' he exclaimed in 1778; 'and several of them very long ones, almost as much as a modern sermon.'[113] Nothing indeed will give us such a high idea of his mental stature or his spiritual maturity as the excellent selection from his correspondence that goes with his biography. They are of the highest order in style and thought, and in point of merit are not a whit behind the best that John Newton ever wrote or published. They are quite free from the faults of his books or his printed sermons, and we feel at once the striking absence of that stiff and laboured mode of expression which mars their usefulness.[114] All his letters are couched in an easy and pleasant style, with a natural and genial freedom from eccentricity which makes us feel that we would gladly hear from such a man again. All his correspondence, like his conversation, was marked by the most lucid simplicity and the most wholesome sincerity; there is a singular union of spiritual joy, rising at times into rapture, with a comprehensive wit, passing at once into judgment. It might have been expected from his extreme warmth of feeling that he would break down in practical decision; but no, nothing is so remarkable as his insight into problems in daily life or Holy Writ.[115] They are steeped in sound and solid Christian faith; they are stored with shrewd and sober common sense. His friends knew that they could place the firmest reliance on his counsel and support in all the exigencies of social life and sinful times; thus his letters to Captain Jonathan Scott and Lady Mary Fitzgerald, with their directions for life and duty, or their solutions of doubt and trouble, are of the first merit. 'I know nothing in the English language of a short kind', quoth Ryle of Venn's Letters, 'so likely to be useful to those who are beginning a Christian life.'[116]

He could be gentle and yet not spare the truth: 'This is one part of the righteous punishment immediately inflicted on those who forsake the Lord after setting their hand to the plough; they can never enjoy, as the unawakened, the pleasures of sin, poor and perishing as they are.'[117] He could be playful, and yet not miss the point: 'I tell her she looks very old, but that word old she cannot endure; yet to be old in the faith is to be near and on the very borders of joy eternal.'[118] He could sum up in a sentence the grand traits of a ripe spiritual experience: 'Oh what a noble independent spirit is produced by the power of godliness!'[119] We catch a glimpse of true domestic happiness as he and his knelt side by side before the Lord's Table: 'There I trust we were united in one faith, one hope, and one Lord, and afresh surrendered ourselves to His service without reserve.'[120] Would we know how he loved to sketch the Pilgrim's Path? 'Things necessary and essential are all plain. The way to heaven is not a bridle-way, winding and difficult to be discerned; but the King's Highway is straight and lifted up, like a Roman road, itself a full direction to the traveller.'[121] Would we know how he chose to paint the Sluggard Soul? 'To pray without attention or without importunity—to pray with our hearts asleep, and worldly thoughts intruding as guests of every character do into an inn-is hypocrisy!'[122] There are pastoral letters which show how tenderly he watched over his flock; there are family letters which show how earnestly he yearned over his home. His letters to his son on the office of the Christian Ministry are a perfect mine of wisdom and goodness; his letters to his daughter on the duties of a domestic character are a noble pattern of fatherly interest and family affection. Rarely indeed does a father succeed in the double task of true Christian faithfulness and of deep familiar affection in his letters to his sons and daughters in the way that good old Henry Venn did.[123] We may pity the man who reads through these letters of long ago, and who does not find his heart strangely warmed; it is an exercise which should fan the flames of true love into a strong fresh blaze of devotion to our Lord and Master.

Henry Venn was as leal and true-hearted a son and servant of the Church of England as she has ever owned. He had inherited the old-fashioned High Churchmanship of his forebears, and he never lost his love and loyalty for the Church in which they had served. But the great change in his heart had brought him over to the despised and obscure sect of so-called Methodists, and his character had made him one of their most distinguished representatives. His new views were more than ever in line with the leading doctrines of the Reformation, and he saw no reason why the Evangelicals should leave the Church while it clung to the Articles and Liturgy compiled by Cranmer and his successors.

Thus he would not tread in Wesley's break-away footsteps when he saw that they would lead in time to a breach with the Church of England; and he ceased to preach in Lady Huntingdon's chapels when a lawsuit put them beyond the pale of the Church of England. He felt that his call was to stand in the line of succession from the Reformers, and he became one of the chief fathers of the Church Evangelicals. His views on these matters were made clear by his love for the Book of Common Prayer; twice, for example, while at Huddersfield, he preached a course of sermons on this subject. 'You and all the people know how I love the Liturgy,' he wrote, 'and would a thousand times prefer it to any other way of worship.'[124] But he took the Bible as his first guide, and his mind was saturated with its truth and spirit. 'Thrice blessed volume,' we hear him say; 'thou art the great deposit once delivered to the saints!...Thou art the charter of all the Church's mercies, and of our hope through eternity!'[125] Venn was both a Churchman and an Evangelical of the first rank, and Ryle does not hesitate in his estimate of his great worth: 'I can put my finger on no leading minister of the century whose views of the gospel appear to have been so truly Scriptural and well-balanced.'[126]

He had begun his work as a zealous Arminian, but his early years at Huddersfield wrought a change in his views. A deep and practical sense of his own unworthiness taught him to ascribe less and less to man's free will; a true and personal proof of God's all-sufficiency taught him to ascribe more and more to His free grace. This soon gave a new tone to his preaching, but he was still far off from the extremes to which many were prone to go. He was singularly reasonable in his regard for the proportions of truth, and he held the doctrines of Grace with a balance and a reserve which were all too rare in that age. His mild reply to a query whether a young man were Calvinist or Arminian in outlook was characteristic: 'I really do not know; he is a sincere disciple of the Lord Jesus Christ, and that is of infinitely more importance than his being a disciple of Calvin or Arminius.'[127] He lived through the storm-ridden 'seventies when the sorry wrangle was at its height and his lifelong friends were drawn up on opposite sides. 'I suppose you have heard of the controversy between Mr Fletcher and Mr Shirley,' he wrote in January 1772; 'who would not wish to be in a lonely village, to be free from such disputes?'[128] He had affirmed his own views long before on the subject of this controversy: 'I...would not give a pin's point to have anyone believe as I do, till the Scriptures by the Spirit's teaching open his understanding.'[129] This he now reaffirmed with his own quiet humour: 'I have always been too much on the side of free grace for many Arminian, too much on the side of experimental religion for many Calvinists.'[130] Thus he would not quarrel with his old friends on such a point, but he spoke out bluntly enough on the theme of Christian Perfection: 'It is an error, built upon false interpretation of some Scripture passages, in flat contradiction to others which cannot be mistaken.... How much more good would Mr Wesley have done, had he not drunk in this error!'[131] But the secret of his strength can be traced in his own words, written within eighteen months of his death:

> I am absolutely certain that I have preached the very doctrine that Christ and His Apostles did. The whole Word of God is equally acceptable to me; not less those parts which are the fortress of Arminians, Perfectionists and Antinomians, than others; so that I am and have been for thirty-five years in the happy state of not being tempted to wrest any Scripture or pervert it in order to make it favour my own tenets.[132]

Venn's fame rests on traditions which are not likely soon to pass away, for his son and his son's sons were all thoroughly likeminded with him; they held the same clear-cut doctrines that he held, and proclaimed them with the same faithful vigour in the hundred years that ensued after his death. Venn brought up his children with a tenderness and a watchfulness that are seldom displayed, and they all turned out well. 'All proved Christians of no common degree, and all gladdened their father's heart in his old age.'[133] One daughter died in infancy, and one lived unmarried to be his right arm in his latter years;

two daughters were married, and one became the mother of Charlotte Elliott. His only son, John, was born in 1758, and was partly educated under Joseph Milner at Hull. He was refused admission to Trinity College in Cambridge, not that he was ignorant, nor that he was dissolute, but because his father was known as an Enthusiast! But in 1777 he went to Sidney Sussex, and in 1781 he took his degree as a Wrangler. In September 1782 he was ordained as a curate to his father at Yelling, and in 1783 he was settled in the Norfolk church of Little Dunham. Here he took as pupils the two sons of Charles Grant, and a little later the sons of Sir Thomas Baring. In September 1789 he married Kitty King, who had been brought up under Joseph Milner, and in 1793 he became Rector of Clapham, after Sir James Stonehouse, who had held the Living for forty years. Thus in July 1793 he was a guest in the home of William Wilberforce, who made a note in his *Diary*: 'I have had Venn with me near a fortnight; he is heavenly-minded, and bent on his Master's work, affectionate to all around him.'[134] Henry Venn's heart rejoiced to see his son stand where he had himself once stood, loved and honoured by all who knew him, a man with clear sight and long vision, who soon mapped out the whole parish for a fresh and vigorous ministry. Neither the mass meetings of his local critics nor the coolness of Church authorities could damp the earnest tone of his sermons or the simple courage of his witness. The Bishop of London would not let his carriage halt at Venn's gate when one of his guests was driven to pay him a visit, for he would not risk his reputation by an open sign of friendship with one who was thought to be a dangerous Jacobin; the good lady had to alight at the Bull's Head, some three hundred yards down the road, and Venn's children were sent to bring her home on foot!

John Venn was a man of quiet culture and shrewd judgment, with strong scientific and literary tastes, whose sensible and sanctified outlook was the very thing for the coterie of friends he found in his parish. Henry Thornton and William Wilberforce, Charles Grant and James Stephen, Lord Teignmouth and Zachary Macaulay, formed a group of laymen whose names had no equal in all England. Good old Henry Venn saw what such a group of men might do. 'May you be more and more united,' he wrote in September 1794, 'and the sons of my old friend (John Thornton), and Mr Wilberforce; and quicken and excite each other to do much in the service of Christ!'[135] The whole Clapham Sect looked up to John Venn as their pastor and guide, and he was thus intimately linked with the thoughts and plans of the good and the wise. He shared their counsels and stimulated their endeavours, both as a friend in their homes and as a pastor in his pulpit. But his own great work was the formation of the Church Missionary Society, and he chaired the vital meeting in the month of April, 1799, when the Society for Missions to Africa and The East came into being. It was he who drew up the first account of the Society for the public, dwelling impressively on the world's need; it was he who drew up the first rules for the new Society, making him the author of its future constitution. It was with true instinct and clear foresight that he laid down the need to found the new Society on the Church principle, unlike the London Missionary Society, but on Evangelical principles, unlike the Society for the Propagation of the gospel. John Venn prepared most of the early documents, drafting rules with remarkable wisdom; and he took part in all the early committees, chairing them as long as health would allow. He preached the Annual Sermon in 1805, and gave the address at the second Farewell Meeting. The Jubilee Statement in 1848 declared that he was 'a man of such wisdom and comprehension of mind that he laid down... those principles and regulations which have formed the basis of the Society.'[136] He fell ill in 1813, and death drew near; he dictated the bulk of his father's *Memoir* from his deathbed, and on July 1, 1813 he passed away to join him in the world above.

John Venn's two sons, Henry and John, were both ordained, and one of them carried the name of Venn to still greater celebrity. Henry Venn the Younger was born on February 10, 1796, two days after Charles Simeon had brought the claims of the heathen world before the Eclectic Society. He was still an infant when old

Henry Venn of Yelling came to end his days at Clapham, but the old man's heart went out to his little grandson and namesake. He loved to hold him in his arms, fondly watching and softly blessing him; and were not all his prayers answered as the child grew when he had been gathered to his fathers? John Venn's home at Clapham was what his own had been in Huddersfield, and few family circles could vie with it for sunny cheerfulness. John's son was only a lad of seventeen at the time of his father's death, but it was then that the lad raised his heart to God and pledged his life to the Saviour.[137] In 1814 he went up to Queens' at Cambridge to be under the aged Isaac Milner, and in 1818 he took his degree as a Wrangler. In 1818 he became a Fellow of Queens', and was ordained by the Bishop of Ely. Two years later he became Curate of St. Dunstan's, Fleet Street, and began to attend meetings at Salisbury Square. In 1824 he returned to Cambridge as Tutor and Proctor, and in 1827 he was presented by Wilberforce to the parish of Drypool near Hull. In 1834 he became Rector of St. John's, Holloway, and in 1841 he was chosen as the Honorary Clerical Secretary of the Church Missionary Society. Four years later he resigned his parish to spend his entire strength for the Society, and the residue of his life and ministry was all absorbed in his work at Salisbury Square. He was a great missionary statesman and strategist, and he holds the first place among the home saints and heroes of the Society. It was Henry Venn who for thirty years had to represent its name before the Church and world, and he had to guide it through some of the most delicate problems and intricate questions it has ever had to confront. He came as an unpaid servant to the Society, and he ruled it in a way that must be unique; but it was the true and legitimate rule of a wise and benevolent master, and it was based on the lessons of an unrivalled experience.

Henry Venn the Younger was a true Evangelical Churchman, and his influence in Evangelical circles was great; but he refused to be merely a party man, and he would not compromise the name of his Society. It is clear that the rich tradition of his grandfather's life and character lived to haunt him like a sacred passion, though his own gifts and his varied talents were so diverse.[138] He was a Prebendary of St. Paul's Cathedral, and a member of two Royal Commissions. In the Commission on Clerical Subscription in 1864 he had to fight for adequate recognition of the Articles as the standard doctrine of the Church of England. In the Commission on Ritual in 1867 he took pains to make a detailed study of the current situation so as to form his own independent judgment. 'Amongst the recompences for the many annoyances of the Ritual Commission,' wrote Dean Stanley, 'I consider one of the greatest was the opportunity it gave me of becoming acquainted with so venerable and beautiful a character.'[139] His life was in fact a model of unwearied industry and practical devotion, with immense powers of application and solid strength of comprehension, with calm and correct judgment, with wise and patient restraint. No name was so identified with the Church Missionary Society in its first hundred years as the name of Venn, and no bearer of that name has left so lasting a mark upon its whole development as Henry Venn. Charles Baring wrote:

> His calm judgment and long-sighted views of results, his firmness and settled opinions upon all doctrinal and ecclesiastical matters, his kindness of heart and manner, his straightforward honesty and candour—all these have won him not merely the confidence of the Committee, but have given him a power with them and an authority which no other Secretary before has ever possessed.[140]

In 1872 he laid down his reins of office as the Honorary Secretary, and was at once made a Vice-President of the Society. This was the highest distinction which the committee could bestow, but a higher comfort to him was to see his son and namesake serving the church of his fathers as Vicar of Walmer. At length, on January 13, 1873, like a shock of ripe corn, he was gathered for the garners of God.

Henry Venn the Elder was a man of singular cheerfulness, in spite of the fact that he had his share of trial in the struggles of ill health and poverty, and the sorrows of sickness and bereavement. He was blessed with a buoyancy and a resilience which helped to bear him up beneath the weight of each fresh cross, and his very portrait was so cheerful that men who did not know him were apt to rate him as a jolly parson of the old school.[141] 'Religious people', he said, 'are heavy, and moping, and cast down, principally because they are idle and selfish.'[142] He himself never knew what it was to spend an idle or vacant hour, or to have a selfish or morbid thought. 'Oh pray for me', he cried, 'that every morning I may rise with an active and steady purpose to be doing something for God!'[143] This strong desire to live for God was matched with the social grace that made him long to live for others; and few men of his age were so free from pique and jealousy, or were so large and catholic in their outlook and affections. He had a quick eye for grace in others, and a ready heart to own it; and his love for Fletcher and Wesley to the end was as warm and true as his love for Berridge and Romaine. Richard Cecil, who knew him well in his last years, used to tell of his way of going on; there was no escape from his warmth! He would meet an old and resolute opponent, and would take him by the arm with all the kindness of a brother, and talk to him about Christ and eternity.[144] But he knew well enough 'how to maintain on fit occasions…a judicial gravity, and even a judicial sternness',[145] and he was a master in the art of advice when called upon to speak his mind. Men of all kinds came to him for counsel, and he gave it without sparing; for he had a well-stored mind and a well-furnished memory, and he was an independent if not original thinker. He was both a preacher at whose voice men wept or trembled, and a friend to whom they turned for help and comfort; he was a guide to the lost and a host for the weary, for he had a rare and noble talent for laying down duty or clearing up doctrine in the light of common sense and gospel glory.

There were indeed few who excelled him in handling vexatious points of moral conduct or difficult facts of credal belief. Sir James Stephen has summed up the reasons which lie behind this fine ability in remarkable words: 'He was one of the most eminent examples of one of the most uncommon of human excellencies—the possession of perfect and uninterrupted mental health.... There prevailed throughout the whole man a certain symphony which enabled him to possess his soul in order, in energy, and in composure.'[146] He was at once a man of deep affection and warm emotion who could act with untiring energy in the press of life, and a man of true devotion and high ambition who could dwell in unwearied solitude with the Word of God.[147] It was his custom at Yelling to spend the hour from six to seven at the close of each day, walking alone, sometimes in the church, sometimes in the house, rapt in solemn prayer or meditation.[148] 'We often are destitute of the spirit of prayer, and therefore find it irksome to bow our knees,' he wrote with regard to his own habit; 'but in this manner of reading the Scriptures, I have seldom failed of finding light and love spring up in my heart.'[149] It is clear that he owed his outward poise in life to an inward peace of heart such as the world never bestows, and his friends still witness to the beautiful character he came to bear. Charles Simeon, who knew him best and had most right to speak of his last years, wrote to John Venn after his death in words that we may well sit and ponder:

> Scarcely ever did I visit him but he prayed with me, at noonday as well as at the common seasons of family worship. Scarcely ever did I dine with him but his ardour in returning thanks, sometimes in an appropriate hymn and sometimes in a thanksgiving prayer, has inflamed the souls of all present so as to give us a foretaste of heaven itself. And in all the years that I knew him, I never remember him to have spoken unkindly of anyone but once; and I was particularly struck with the humiliation which he expressed for it in his prayer the next day.[150]

Was not Henry Venn a noble illustration of his own fine remark: 'An old disciple who has always walked uprightly is one of the finest sights upon earth'?[151]

Old age set in prematurely for Henry Venn, although his life had been spared far beyond its first expectations. In September 1785 his health was low, and fears for his life were entertained. 'Blessed be God!' he exclaimed; 'my trust is in the blood and righteousness of Jesus Christ, in His promises and Covenant, and all is well!'[152] But by January 1786 he was up and active once more, and could tell his children: 'I have begun again to have the people one night in the week; near fifty come.'[153] He still spent a few weeks each summer in London, when he used to preach in Surrey Chapel. These short visits to the City were hailed by his friends with unmixed delight, and his genial company was a power for good in the London circles of life and thought to the very close of the century. Thus, in May 1786, he made a note of one of his London hearers: 'Mr Wilberforce has been at the Chapel, and attends the preaching constantly.'[154] He kept up these yearly visits till June 1790, but that was the last time when he could be induced to preach: 'My work is nearly ended,' he wrote; 'for my mental faculties are very dull, and my bodily strength greatly reduced.'[155] He had remarked of his elder brother only a month or two before: 'Amazingly strong is our love of life, even of the very dregs of life!'[156] But he was near the dregs of life himself, and the close of the year left him ill and prostrate. 'I am come to the days of darkness, but not of dejection,' he wrote; 'for why should not Christians be afraid of dejection, as they are of murmuring and complaining?'[157] He felt that the time had come to do less, and in the autumn of 1791 he engaged a curate for Yelling. He was hardly equal to the smallest duties, and his friends were alarmed to see the change. Thus in July 1791 Newton went to see him at Yelling, and was grieved to find him old and feeble.[158] 'I am sorry that Mr Venn's labours below are so near to a conclusion,' Cowper wrote at this same time to Newton; 'I have seen few men whom I could have loved more, had opportunity been given me to know him better. So at least I have thought, as often as I have seen him.'[159]

In the summer months of 1792 he was obliged to cease from all public duties, and to pay a visit to Bath in search of health. He was away from Yelling for more than twelve months,[160] and on his return was shut up to his house for a further year and a half.[161] 'I have not slept out of my house or been farther than my garden and the adjoining fields,' he wrote in January 1795, 'for more than eighteen months; yet I enjoy liberty. I soar to heaven, and mix in the society of cherubim and seraphim, and all the ransomed of the Lord.'[162] Thomas Haweis found his memory as strong and his faculties as fresh as they ever had been, and all his soul alert to things sacred and divine.[163] Daniel Wilson as a very young man was most impressed when he once saw Venn led into the pew next to his own to hear Romaine not long before Romaine's death in 1795.[164] On New Year's Day in January 1796 he wrote to his son in the last of his published letters: 'I have to tell you, and would if it were with my last breath, that I can wish for nothing more than I now find Christ is to me.'[165] Charles Simeon still watched over him as a son over his father, and in October 1796 he wrote with tender solicitude: 'Dear Mr Venn is much as usual; if his eye waxes dim, his heart does not wax cold. God is very abundantly gracious unto him.'[166] Three months later he felt that the time had come to lay down sword and trowel for good and all, and he left Yelling to go and live with his son at Clapham. Six months of life were still his to enjoy, though his health was precarious indeed, and he renewed his now lifelong fellowship with the Thornton family in the parish of his early labours. He was constantly occupied in reading or writing, in meditation or intercession, and while he had once spent one hour a day in prayer he now spent three or four.[167] The spread of Christ's Kingdom on earth seemed to absorb his thoughts and lie nearer to his heart than any concerns of his own; and did not this become the last of that first great generation of those who had been in the van of the Evangelical Revival? He was not so apostolic as Grimshaw, nor so original as Berridge; not so polished as Romaine, nor so rugged as Newton; not so laconic as Wesley, nor so seraphic as Fletcher. But he was a fellow servant who ranked high in that great company, the intimate friend of Whitefield in his early years, the favourite guide of Simeon in his riper age, a great man and a good. But Wesley had fallen asleep in 1791, and Berridge in 1793, and Romaine in 1795; and his own sun was now about to set in a calm bright evening. Yet the very prospect of his dissolution and the glory beyond so filled his mind with joy and elation that it proved a stimulus to life. 'Sir,' said his medical adviser, 'in this state of joyous excitement, you cannot die!'[168] At length, on June 24, 1797, at the age of 73, his blithe and blessed spirit reached that other shore where the tide of joy flows calm and deep and full, and ebbs no more.

Bibliography

John Venn and Henry Venn, *The Life and a Selection from the Letters of the Late Rev. Henry Venn*, M.A. (1837).

William Knight, *Memoir of Henry Venn, B.D., Hon. Sec. of C.M.S.* (1883).

John Venn, *Annals of a Clerical Family* (1904.).

Henry Venn, *The Complete Duty of Man.*

John Charles Ryle, 'Henry Venn and His Ministry', Chapter IX in *Christian Leaders of the Last Century* (New Ed., 1880).

'A Member of the Houses of Shirley and Hastings', *The Life and Times of Selina, Countess of Huntingdon* (1839).

Luke Tyerman, *The Life and Times of the Rev. John Wesley* (4th Ed., 1878).

Luke Tyerman, *The Life of The Rev. George Whitefield* (2nd Ed., 1890).

Luke Tyerman, *Wesley's Designated Successor: Fletcher of Madeley* (1882).

Luke Tyerman, *The Oxford Methodists* (1878).

Nehemiah Curnock, *The Journal of the Rev. John Wesley, A.M.* (Bicentenary Issue, 1938).

Thomas Haweis, *The Life of William Romaine, M.A.* (1797).

Edwin Sidney, *The Life of the Rev. Rowland Hill, A.M.* (1834).

Josiah Bull, *John Newton* (2nd Ed., 1868).

William Carus, *Memoirs of the Life of the Rev. Charles Simeon, M.A.* (1847)

Handley C. G. Moule, *Charles Simeon* ('Leaders of Religion' Series, 1892).

Charles Smyth, *Simeon and Church Order* (1940).

Josiah Bateman, *The Life of the Rev. Daniel Wilson, D.D.* (1860).

James Stephen, *Essays in Ecclesiastical Biography* (New Ed., 1875).

Eugene Stock, *The History of The Church Missionary Society* (1899).

G. R. Balleine, *A History of the Evangelical Party* (New Ed., 1933)

'The name, the influence, which characterises most deeply and broadly the Evangelicism of the first third of the century, in the ranks of the Christian ministry, is certainly that of Charles Simeon....He was a great power for God...in the pure truth of his life, the noble sobriety of his fervour, the manly wisdom of his teaching, his immense diligence in every duty, his total freedom from selfish aims, and the human warmth of his heart.'

H. C. G. Moule
The Evangelical School in the Church of England, 8–9

4

Charles Simeon
1759–1836

Charles Simeon was born at Reading on 24 September 1759, the
fourth and youngest son in a house of ancient lineage. His birth
took place in the same year as that of his lifelong friend and
fellow-Cantabrigian, William Wilberforce, and his life was to
stretch from the last days of George II to the last months of
William IV. His father was the son and grandson of successive
incumbents of a Berkshire Living, and his mother was the
daughter of a family which had supplied two Archbishops to the
Northern Province. It would seem that the death of his mother
must have occurred in his early childhood, and he grew up
without the care which she alone could have supplied. His father
was an upright man who had more of deference than of affection
from his sons, and who held the Church in formal respect rather
than in vital esteem. In 1767, when not quite eight years old,
Charles was sent to the Royal College of Eton, and in 1773 he was
admitted to the Foundation. Rowland Hill had left the school in
1764, three years before his time, and his little group of Christian
followers had been dispersed in the meanwhile. Eton in those

days was by no means a nursery of virtue, but he was strict both in life and habit as a schoolboy. He was never handsome, and his youthful looks were whimsically ugly; he was nicknamed 'Chin' Simeon, and he sought some compensation in dress and in other minor personal vanities. His main faults were in the way of undisciplined temper and extravagant taste, but a certain lack of general convention gave him as well a slight air of oddity. Otherwise, he was a normal boy with strong athletic interests and a flair for strenuous exercise; and in particular he could ride, judge and handle a horse with as much ease and dexterity as if he had been born and bred in the dales of Yorkshire.

In January 1779 he went up to Cambridge in the footsteps of his elder brothers, and was enrolled as a scholar of King's. He had come up with a scant enough store of Greek, but he had been well drilled in the Latin Classics; and in Cambridge, through ill report and good report, he was to spend the whole of life that still remained. Rowland Hill had taken his degree in 1769, ten years before, and no voice like his had since been raised in fearless spiritual testimony with the same wide appeal; but his mantle was to fall on Simeon's broad shoulders, and a vast change was to transform the whole scene in Simeon's own lifetime. He came to a Cambridge which was still rich in the tradition of Newton and Bentley; he passed from a Cambridge which was just fresh to the impetus of Whewell and Sedgwick. He came as a Freshman at a time when university life had sunk to a disgracefully low level both in letters and in morals; he died as a Fellow at a time when undergraduate thought had climbed to a remarkably high plateau both in learning and in virtue. The waves of the great Evangelical Movement in the century on the wane had left Cambridge almost untouched; there was nothing that could even remotely correspond to the Holy Club at Oxford at the time when Simeon went up. The strength of the great Evangelical Movement in the century just at hand was to flow from Cambridge almost alone; it had produced the most wisely successful counterpart to the Newman school at Oxford by the time when Simeon passed on. No one was to contribute more to this salutary change than Simeon himself, and the change in Cambridge as a whole was exemplified in the initial transformation which took place in his own experience. The first great step was then at hand.

Within three days of his advent to King's an incident occurred which in the will of God was to change his entire future. He received a message from the Provost to the effect that the Service of Holy Communion would be held at mid-term, and that he would have to attend as a communicant. This was based on an old College rule which has long since been repealed, but it took him by shock and surprise. There on his table lay the cold, formal notice; he, careless youth, would have to present himself at this sacred rite of worship and kneel where he had never knelt before. The whole situation took on the hue of an awful solemnity as seen by his trembling conscience. 'What! said I, *must* I attend? On being informed that I must, the thought rushed into my mind that Satan himself was as fit to attend as I; and that if I must attend, I must *prepare* for my attendance there.'[1] He began with tremendous earnestness to comb the past and to mourn its misdeeds; he set out to undo the harm of all erstwhile sins as far as he could. Three weeks of reading, fasting, and praying, left him ill and prostrate, but taught him that the salvation of his own soul was the one thing needful. Three months later he was still in distress, knowing that he would have to kneel before the Lord's Table again on Easter Day. But at length he fell in with a little book by Bishop Wilson of the Isle of Man which pointed him to the Cross, just as Evangelist pointed Bunyan's Pilgrim to the light that shone clear beyond the gloomy fields. He was reading it in Passion Week when he met with a remark to the effect that the Hebrew sinner knew what he was about when he transferred his sin to the head of the beast he was ready to slay; and the light broke with that remark!

His own graphic words tell the tale as no other words can ever aspire to do:

The thought rushed into my mind, What! may I transfer all my guilt to another? Has God provided an offering for me that I may lay my sins on His head? Then, God willing, I will not bear them on my own soul one moment longer. Accordingly, I sought to lay my sins upon the sacred Head of Jesus, and on the Wednesday began to have a hope of mercy; on the Thursday that hope increased; on the Friday and Saturday it became more strong; and on the Sunday morning, Easter Day, April 4, I awoke early with those words upon my heart and lips, Jesus Christ is risen to-day! Hallelujah! Hallelujah! From that hour peace flowed in rich abundance into my soul; and at the Lord's Table in our Chapel, I had the sweetest access to God through my blessed Saviour.[2]

Thus he who had been far off was made nigh by the blood of Christ; one who was a stranger to grace had been made a servant of God. Never did he lose sight of the atoning sacrifice in years to come; he loved to look back to that glad—Easter morning when first he saw the light.[3] He could not think of the death of the Lord Jesus except as the death of his Substitute Sin-bearer, and it was to this that he owed all his sense of peace and freedom. In the massive volume of Brown's *Self-Interpreting Bible* which was his lifelong companion, special attention is drawn to one verse: 'That thou mayest remember the day when thou camest forth out of the land of Egypt all the days of thy life' (Deut. 16: 3). In the margin, with the hand of old age, he wrote and underlined this one pregnant remark: 'So must I, and God helping me, so will I, the Easter week, and especially the Easter Sunday, when my deliverance was complete!'[4]

The most powerful of all incentives for a life of duty and service now took full possession of Simeon's energetic will, and he held on his way with a perseverance which never flagged after that first critical term. King's men in those days were exempt from all university examinations, and promotion to fellowships was governed by routine as due to the senior members of the College. Simeon became a Fellow of King's in January 1782, though he did not take his degree for a further twelve months; and then he was ordained on his title as a Fellow in May 1782, though he was still four months short of the canonical age. His work began as a curate in St. Edward's Church, where he occupied 'good old Latimer's pulpit',[5] with all the martyred bishop's power for direct and earnest appeal. Within four months the church was filled with new hearers, and the communicants had trebled in number; 'a thing unknown there for near a century', as good old Henry Venn exclaimed.[6] 'He preaches at a church in the town,' wrote Berridge to Newton on September 17, 'which is crowded like a theatre on the first night of a new play.'[7] Then, in October, he was called to watch by the death-bed of his eldest brother, and he thankfully saw his life reach its close in peace. But this death left a gap in his home which he thought duty called him to fill, and he was just on the point of leaving Cambridge when a new and pressing call came. He had often walked past the Church of the Holy Trinity which stands by the market in the very heart of Cambridge, and he would think within himself: 'How should I rejoice if God were to give me that church that I might preach His gospel there, and be a herald for Him in the midst of the University!'[8] And so at length it was to be.

It was a dream which had seemed as remote from him as the See of Canterbury, but God gave him all his desire. The church happened to fall vacant just at this time, and the bishop's friendship with his father led to Simeon's appointment while he was only as yet in Deacon's Orders. But the parishioners were anxious to secure the appointment for a nominee of their own, whom they had already elected to the Sunday afternoon lectureship. This led to a severe trial for Simeon, but he followed the line of prudence and patience. He was willing to withdraw in favour of the popular nominee rather than split the whole parish in two; but the parishioners overreached themselves. The Bishop of Ely was so incensed by their conduct that he told Simeon that the church was his if he would have it; but in no circumstances would he give it to his rival. This cut the knot, and cleared his conscience; he resolved to accept the charge as in the sight of Him who sees the soul, and his first sermon was preached a day later, on November 10, 1782. His task was so to preach that God might use him to evangelize town and gown in Cambridge, and this bright sense of his call and mission was to distinguish his whole ministry. Thus was launched, a life of toil for four-and-fifty years with many vicissitudes of weal and woe, a life which was to make his church a source of radiant light for gownsmen and the sons of gownsmen; thus he began to wield the power of such old-time giants as Richard Sibbes and Thomas Goodwin who had exercised their strong Puritan ministry from the selfsame pulpit, a power which was once more to make the church ring with Scriptural enterprise in the very heart of Cambridge.

Simeon owed his soul to the grace of God, altogether apart from human aid, and for three years he stood alone in his college life and witness. He longed for a friend with whom to share his views and feelings,[9] but he had never been in the company of a decided Christian up to the time of his ordination.[10] At length, in June 1782, he met in John Venn of Sidney Sussex one who was to become a lifelong friend. 'Here I found a man after my own heart,' he wrote when Venn died in 1813; 'a man for whom...I ever shall retain the most affectionate remembrance.'[11] They first met and drank tea on June 1, but they saw each other five times within the first week that followed. Then John Venn left Cambridge for his home at Yelling, some twelve miles away to the west. On June 13 Simeon walked over to Yelling to visit John Venn, whose father and sisters were then away from home; on June 14 John Venn took him over to Everton, and introduced him to Berridge. Four or five weeks later he rode back to Yelling to meet John Venn's father, the famous Henry Venn, one of the choicest names in the story of the Church of England. He arrived soon after eight in the morning, and remained till after eight in the evening. Not one detail of that long summer day has been preserved, but Simeon's brief exclamation may still be read in his *Memoir*: 'O, what an acquisition was this! In this aged minister, I found a father, an instructor, and a most bright example; I shall have reason to adore my God to all eternity for the benefit of his acquaintance.'[12] It was the dawn of a friendship between youth and old age which left the most profound impress on his character and his ministry; all that good old Berridge had been to Rowland Hill, Henry Venn was now to become for Simeon.

Many a morning he walked or rode across the then almost hedgeless fields from Cambridge to Yelling; six times he made the short journey within the first three months.[13] Henry Venn's heart was drawn to him with rare trust and delight. 'He is calculated for great usefulness, and is full of faith and love,' he wrote on October 9, 1782; 'my soul is always the better for his visits. Oh, to flame as he does with zeal, and yet be beautified with meekness!'[14] Once when he rode away from one of these early visits, Venn's three daughters began to pass comments on his manner. The old man led them out to the garden, and asked them to bring him a peach. But it was still early summer, and the time of fruit was not yet. How could he ask for a green peach? 'Well,' he said, 'it is green now, and we must wait; but a little more sun and a few more showers, and the peach will be ripe and sweet. So it is with Mr Simeon!'[15] As for Simeon, his love for the Venns at Yelling grew till it was like a sacred passion; the son was his trusted friend and confidant, while the father was his honoured guide and counsellor. In the holy wisdom and kindly humour of Henry Venn, in his vast wealth of strong faith and good sense, in his genial character and natural affection, he found help and guidance at many anxious turns in the first years of a difficult ministry. Forty years later he wrote to one of Venn's grandsons: 'In the efforts of a thousand years, I never can repay my obligations to him for all his labours of love.'[16] And, in 1833, to a second grandson he wrote: 'I wish you had known your honoured grandfather; the only end for which he lived was to make all men see the glory of God in the face of Jesus Christ.'[17]

Simeon soon found himself in sore need of all the help the Venns could give him, for he was faced with serious difficulty and strenuous opposition from town and gown alike. Belligerent parishioners were in the mood for war; long and painful was the conflict which they set out to wage against his life and ministry. He was denied the use of his pulpit on the Sunday afternoon by the choice of someone else as special lecturer, and twelve years had to pass away before this task fell into his own hands. He was not free to do as he might wish even at the morning service, for the church was made as inaccessible as they could contrive. The seatholders locked the doors of their pews so that no one could use them, and then left the church in a body. Simeon placed forms in the aisles and seats in the nooks at his own expense, but the wardens dragged them out and threw them into the street. The aisles were almost as empty as the pews on his first Sunday when the service began, but the people trooped in before it was over. 'In this state of things', he wrote, 'I saw no remedy but faith and patience.'[18] The passage of Scripture which subdued and controlled his own mind was never very far from his thoughts: 'The servant of the Lord must not strive' (2 Tim. 2: 24). He went over to consult with Henry Venn at each fresh crisis, but the Wonderful Counsellor was with him too.[19] His friends had no fear that he would fail in energetic courage; a gracious God would see that he did not fail in long-suffering wisdom. 'Mr Simeon's ministry is likely to be blessed,' wrote Venn in February 1783; 'many gownsmen hear him.'[20] 'I have good news to send you from Cambridge,' he wrote in the following January. 'Mr Simeon is made for great usefulness.'[21] Two years later, in January 1786, he could cheer Rowland Hill with the report: 'Mr Simeon's character shines brightly; he grows in humility, is fervent in spirit, and very bountiful and loving.'[22]

Meanwhile the news of his appointment had been welcomed by his growing circle of friends, and he was sustained all through the first ten years of trial by their prayerful love and counsel. Through his friendship with the Venns he had come into contact with some of the greatest figures in the Evangelical world; they were all veterans in the fight, and they saw in him a valiant successor. He was received by quaint John Berridge and bluff John Newton; he had conversed with the aged Wesley and the saintly Fletcher. Wesley saw in him a kindred soul with Fletcher in his warmth of spirit and his wealth of address; when he met him again, shortly before his death, he wrote of him as one who breathed 'the very spirit of Mr Fletcher'.[23] There were also visits to men like Thomas Scott and Richard Cecil; there were letters from men like John Thornton and William Romaine. 'The Lord sees fit to fix you in a noble stand indeed,' wrote John Newton in November 1782; 'He has chosen for you, and on Him therefore you may confidently rely.'[24] 'Thou art called to be a man of war from thy youth,' wrote Henry Venn in December 1783; 'may the Captain of our Salvation be thy Guide, Shield, and Strength.'[25] After many weeks of patient waiting he began an evening lecture with a six-o'clock service and an unwritten address so that he might occupy the pulpit twice each Sunday. This was an almost unheard of innovation, and it drew large congregations for the first few Sundays; then the wardens locked the church and carried off the keys while they all stood in the street. This was as illegal as it was uncivil, but he felt that it would be wise to let it drop until the next summer. 'May God bless them', Simeon prayed, 'with enlightening, sanctifying, and saving grace.'[26] As weeks wore on there was scarcely room to contain those who wished to attend; but for ten years they had to stand in the aisles while the pews were bare. Even then there was a small party who kept the old animosities alive, and traces of opposition still remained even after thirty years. Then they ceased, and he was held at last in love and veneration by all.

He had to meet opposition no less severe in more academic circles, and this was perhaps harder still to bear. He soon learnt what it meant to be known as an Evangelical by his contemporaries, for he was met by men in his own line of life with cool contempt. Isaac Milner of Queens', and William Farish of Magdalene, were in essential agreement with him; but these three were almost alone of their order. Cambridge Fellows as a whole looked on him with doubt and suspicion, and he had to endure 'the slow trials of social estrangement'.[27] He was so snubbed that it even seemed too much to expect one of the Fellows in his own College to take his arm and walk beside him on the wide smooth lawns of King's.[28] He was for long slandered and maligned as a bad man who made a high profession of goodness; but it was in fact his fearless message which lay at the root of this reproach and persecution. It was part of the offence of the Cross; but that was an article of faith for the Christian which had long been buried in dark oblivion. It was the relative novelty of his message which gave such point to its searching demands, and the human heart in its pride rebelled.[29] Sargent affirms, in his *Life of Thomas Thomason*, that those who went much to Trinity were thought 'to have left common sense, discretion, sobriety, attachment to the Established Church, love of the Liturgy, and whatever else is true and of good report, in the vestibule'.[30] But though Fellows would hold aloof, gownsmen were sure to flock in the direction of Trinity and Simeon for good or ill. Was he not a Fellow of King's, and had he not won a reputation as a preacher? He was at war with his parish, and he was known as an Evangelical! That was enough to draw gownsmen in crowds from the outset.

They soon came in rowdy bands whose one aim was to disturb and to annoy. Even in their College Chapels they showed little more reverence for God than if they were in a play-house,[31] and at Holy Trinity there were wild scenes of riot and tumult, with filth and stones freely flung on all sides. One eye-witness relates how he saw Simeon on his way back to King's, his face and clothes streaming with rotten eggs which had been hurled at him as he left the church.[32] But this only served to challenge and call forth his courage, and he dealt with offenders with a strong hand. The firmness of his conduct and the texture of his sermons helped him to win the fight, and many who came only to annoy found themselves constrained to remain for worship. Once he fixed his stern eyes on two young men who had entered the church in most disorderly fashion. One of them was abashed before that gaze, but the other returned look for look with cool and complete effrontery; he not only refused to drop his eyes, but he was the only man who ever dared to try to stare him out. In the morning Simeon sent for him and charged him with the extreme folly of his conduct; he warned him Who it was that he had thus defied, and then forbade him to enter the church again unless he was prepared to come with a very different attitude. To his surprise he was present the next Sunday morning, though with a more becoming demeanour, and from then on he continued to come until it pleased God to open his eyes and to lead him into the truth. A year or two later he turned from the study of Law to be ordained as a preacher of the faith he had once despised, and he became one of Simeon's favourites in his inmost circle of friends.[33] This was Sargent, whom he named as his 'dearest friend...on earth' after the death of Henry Martyn and Thomas Thomason.[34]

Meanwhile his growth in the balanced wisdom of a practical ministry went on apace, largely owing to the firm guidance of Henry Venn. The real turning-point came in June 1785 while Venn was away from home in London, for it was then that he began to preach in a barn at Bluntisham. But this was as much a cause of distress to Venn as it was a source of satisfaction to John Berridge, and he wrote from London to put an end to it at once. It was one thing for Venn and for Berridge to have ignored the rules of Church Order; it was quite another thing for young Simeon to imitate their example at the outset of his promising ministry. Berridge had made Rowland Hill a second Berridge, but Venn would not let Simeon itinerate; he put a stop to his irregular preaching, and taught him to develop his full ministry within the pale of the Church of England.[35] Venn was far more content to watch his growth in grace, and the autumn of that same year found him writing that he was the only one of all the Cambridge men who wholly followed the Lord as did Caleb.[36] 'Mr Simeon's light shines brighter and brighter,' he told Rowland Hill in 1786; 'he is highly esteemed, and exceedingly despised; almost adored by some, and by others abhorred.'[37] 'Very few are so exemplary in their walk as he is,' he affirmed in 1787; 'and none can bear and receive profit from reproof like himself.'[38] It would seem that he could never wholly suppress the quick temper and the innocent vanity which had characterized him as a lad, and as late as 1827 the author of *Alma Mater* was to recount how the 'old cushion-thumper' rode on the Gogmagogs, leaping ditches and making his servant follow; and when he failed to take a ditch in the Senior Wrangler's Walk the old preacher thundered at him: 'You cowardly dog, why don't you follow?'[39] But John Venn said that his very presence was a blessing,[40] and his father declared that his visits never failed to leave a blessing behind when he himself had gone.[41]

The path which Simeon tried to follow had been marked out very plainly by the finger of God, and he held on his way with the undeviating care and disinterested love of absolute loyalty. He proved himself by the manly wisdom of his conduct, by the sober balance of his fervour, by his total freedom from selfish aims, by the patient courage of his public life. But this was the golden fruit of a strong inner life which was hid with Christ in God; he was sustained all through those years of trial by the secret of an unfettered reliance on Him. Behind all that was busy or trying in his public life he strove from the first to labour in prayer. One who shared his rooms for a time in those early years could never forget how he invariably rose from his bed at four in the morning, even in the coldest winter, to light a fire and then to spend four long hours in prayer and Bible study.[42] Here lay the real secret of his great grace and spiritual strength; but it was a habit which he had had to fight hard to acquire, and more hardly still to retain. Early rising did not come more easily to him than to others, but he resolved to pay a self-imposed fine of half a crown to his bed-maker each time he was guilty of some failure. But the morning came when he caught himself thinking that she was poor, and could well do with half a crown if he were to remain in bed. That was a fallacy he dared not tolerate, and he resolved that if he slept long and rose late again, he would throw a sovereign into the Cam. Only once did he fail to rise, and for his Lord's sake the coin was cast into the Cam. There no doubt it lies yet, in the river's keeping; but he never transgressed in the same way again.[43] He had learnt the art of regular discipline for self, and it had set his feet on the path of intimate communion with God.

But this interior life of prayer was based on the most zealous study of Holy Writ. He pored long and reverently over each sacred page in his longing to know the will of God and to share the mind of Christ in all things. 'God does draw nigh to the soul that seeks Him in His Word, and does communicate an unction that is in vain sought for in the books of men,' he wrote; 'and that unction will, like the ointment of the right hand, bewray itself, both in the pulpit and out of it.'[44] He drew his views of truth from the Scriptures alone, and he adhered to the letter of the Book with scrupulous loyalty; 'never wresting any portion of the Word of God to favour a particular opinion, but giving every part of it that sense which it seems...to have been designed by its Great Author to convey.'[45] He shared with old Henry Venn a profound veneration for the Book of Common Prayer, just because he found that it was soaked in the spirit and steeped in the language of the Bible. Its prayers had been like 'marrow and fatness' to his own soul after his conversion, even though read with careless drone or drowsy voice.[46] He had no thought for the wooden spirit of a lifeless reader, unless it were thoughts of wistful pity; his soul was lost in the awe and wonder that soared on the wings of worship to the Throne of Grace and Glory. It was pure joy for him to lead his flock in the forms of worship laid down in the Liturgy; he could never feel that he was nearer to God than he often felt in the Reading Desk. 'If all men could pray at all times as some men can sometimes', he would observe, 'then indeed we might prefer extempore to precomposed prayers.'[47] But in view of all the infirmities of our human nature, he felt that they are blessed who have a Prayer Book so rich in Scriptural truth and teaching.

Simeon's churchmanship was thus primarily controlled by his love for the whole English Bible, and this gave its colour to all his wide range of activity. His aim was to see each fragment of truth in its right perspective, and then to hold the whole body of truth in its right proportion. 'My endeavour', he used to say, 'is to bring out of Scripture what is there, and not to thrust in what I think might be there.'[48] Thus it was his settled plan in preaching to expound the Scripture as clearly and closely as he could, and then to bring its message to bear in full weight and power on heart and conscience. But the root of this love for the Word of God lay deep down in his own soul, and he himself has left us the record of one item from his personal history which makes this clear. In one crisis of his earlier ministry, when he felt hard pressed by the cold disdain of the College Fellows and was in doubt as to how far duty required him to carry on in Cambridge, he strolled forth with his Greek Testament in his hand. He was in great distress of mind, but he offered earnest prayer that God would comfort him with some plain verse from Scripture. Then he opened his Greek Testament in the Epistles, as he thought; but he did not notice that the book was upside down, and so fell open at the Gospels. Thus the text on which his finger lay was one which came with complete surprise: 'And as they came out, they found a man of Cyrene, Simon by name; him they compelled to bear His cross' (Matt. 27: 32). At once the thought flashed through his mind that Simon was the same as Simeon, and a hint was enough! To have the cross laid on him that he might bear it after Jesus, what a privilege! 'And when I read that', he wrote, 'I said, Lord, lay it on me, lay it on me; I will gladly bear the cross for Thy sake!'[49] Thus he bound the thorns of persecution as a wreath of glory round his brow, glad to share in the fellowship of His sufferings.

Full of difficulty and trial as Simeon's pastoral cares were in the first year, he ceased not to do good and strive for souls. He felt that he had begun to win a foothold in the parish by the winter of 1786,[50] and he was able to start the evening lecture with the consent of his wardens in the summer of 1790.[51] He carried on his ministry to the congregation in the church aisles until 1794, when at length the afternoon lectureship passed into his hands and the doors of the church pews were unlocked.[52] His whole style of address, grave and candid, had been signally free from that easy mistake and fatal pitfall of troubled ministers, a chiding accent and scolding spirit.[53] He had the right note to conciliate those who were least opposed, and not a few were led by his preaching to seek for more personal contact with him as their pastor. He had done his best to organize the life and work of the parish, and he had seen the need for close pastoral oversight if his converts were not to drift. This had induced him to hire a room where he could assemble his flock for non-church meetings in what he called a society; the society grew as his acceptance in the parish grew, and a larger room was taken in the next-door parish when the first room proved quite inadequate. This was irregular in point of law; it might have been classed as a forbidden conventicle. But though it was the one flank which really exposed him to attack, no voice was ever raised against him on that score.[54] It was in these society meetings that he found his great chance to meet men and women at close quarters, and by the year 1794 there were more than one hundred souls whom the Lord had called and blessed by this means.[55]

Thus he won through by the faith and patience that kept his soul, and life began to move at last in calmer channels and kinder circles. He and Henry Venn used to go over and dine with John Berridge at Everton every Tuesday, and these visits were often the staple of some reminiscence in years to come.[56] But in 1793 he was called upon to preach the funeral sermon for good old Berridge,[57] and in 1797 he had to mourn the death of Venn whom he had loved only less than the Lord Himself.[58] But in 1796 he secured the appointment of Thomas Thomason to share his labours as friend and colleague, and this set him free to leave his parish both in 1796 and in 1798 for two prolonged tours of Scotland. He set out to travel through the Highlands at a time when horseback was the only means of transport, and his journey, like that of the gruff old Johnson with his Boswell for guide, was a far more venturesome enterprise than we can now conceive. He preached from a Scottish pulpit on each Scottish Sabbath, and great numbers came to hear him. He found himself opposed, not by English Churchmen, but by Scottish Moderates, just as Whitefield had been by the Erskine Secession. It led to an Act which was passed by the General Assembly in 1799 to debar strangers from all Scottish pulpits, and this Act shut Rowland

Hill out of all northern churches on his later tour of Scotland. Simeon took part in more than one Scottish Communion in a spirit of deep and reverent devotion. 'I made a free, full, and unreserved surrender of myself to God,' he wrote after the service at Stirling on June 19, 1796; 'O that I may ever bear in mind His kindness to me, and my obligations to Him!'[59] These two northern visits marked him out as the best and most valuable link between English and Scottish churchmen since George Whitefield, and gave him fresh ardour and momentum for his pastoral cares in Trinity on his return thither.

But it was through the university that his influence was to permeate the whole English Church with profound effect. The wall of prejudice which had faced him at first was slowly broken down, though hostile feeling was sustained in some quarters for long, long years. But things were at their worst in the 'eighties, when few could be found who would speak kindly of him; he was falsely accused by rumour and slander, and was grossly maligned by reproach and contempt. But these were obstacles which he had overcome, and the academic world at Cambridge was at length taught how to recognize his real worth and character. He had made his weight felt almost from the first as a guide for young gownsmen, and his prestige as a friend and teacher grew with the years. Perhaps the year 1786 marked the turn of the tide, for in that year he preached his first sermon before the University in the Church of Great St. Mary's. His call to this duty at a time when he was still so young and far from popular may seem strange, but it was due to the anomalies which then prevailed in the choice of preachers. He was often to preach from that pulpit in his later career, and the church was seldom so full as when he was known to be the preacher. But it is safe to say that the attraction for the curious was never stronger than it was on that first occasion. Gownsmen came in crowds to provoke and annoy, and he faced a critical and prejudiced audience. But his enemies were as astonished as his friends were delighted, for he was heard to the end with the most impressive attention. Subdued remarks as the people dispersed still disclose the surprise and the seriousness which his sermon provoked. One man was heard to say: 'Well! Simeon is no fool!' 'Fool!' replied his friend; 'did you ever hear such a sermon before?'[60]

He now found himself able to play an active part in College duties, and he long held office in one capacity or another at King's. From 1788-1790 he was Dean of Arts or Divinity; from 1790 to 1792 he was the Vice-Provost of his College. From 1790 to 1798 he held one or other of the Deanships; from 1798 to 1805 he was Second Bursar for the College. He brought credit to each office in turn, and this record helped to arm him with a solid moral authority in the eyes of junior members of King's. But his main work in the student world was carried out by means of private meetings held for gownsmen in his own rooms, for this brought him into closer touch with them than any other form of contact. If there were a vein of explosive oddity in him as an old man, it had served its own end as an eccentric attraction for those who so gladly came to his rooms for fellowship and instruction. There is no clear record of the origin of this ministry, but by 1790 he had begun to hold meetings in his rooms on Sunday evenings. This was the first blossom of a unique movement which he firmly planted in the heart of Cambridge, and it was to flower in many colours as he cultivated it in the years to come. Thus in 1792 he began the Sermon Classes, which were confined to the future ordinands; and in 1812 he convened the Conversation Parties, which were designed for all student visitors.[61] There were special groups which he held for the study of Scripture; there were other groups which he took for the study of Doctrine. They were schools of manly thought and common sense in dealing with the problems of young men on the great issues of life and truth. Men like Martyn and Thomason, Sargent and Sowerby, never knew more of the communion of saints on earth than in his rooms at such meetings.[62] They have become famous with the passage of time, for the men who passed through his rooms were the spearhead of the Evangelical Movement in the nineteenth century; and the meetings which he began with weakness and trembling in those early years of conflict were developed for nearly fifty years with results 'which no man can estimate'.[63]

It was the great glory of Charles Simeon that he combined local strength in Cambridge with an imperial outlook on the need of the world.[64] In 1786 David Brown had sailed for Calcutta as a chaplain with the British East India Company, and had found in Charles Grant a devoted friend in the things of God. A year later, with two other laymen, they wrote to ask Simeon if he would act as their agent, and would help them to find suitable volunteers for a mission which they hoped to found at Benares. Nothing came of this plan at the time on account of the hostility of the great merchant company; but it forged an alliance between Grant and Simeon which was to pave the way for a still more productive enterprise. They were for doing good on a truly noble scale, and their dreams were to be wrought out in sober fact and solid reality. Charles Grant joined the Board of Company Directors on his return home in 1790, and he took up the whole case for missionary effort both at Lambeth Palace and at Windsor Castle. But his plan for a State Mission was lost in the House of Commons by the vote of 1793, and the result was that William Carey and his friends could only live and work in Danish territory. It was largely through the efforts of the Clapham Sect that an Act to set up the Calcutta Bishopric was passed by Parliament in 1813, and the company territories were at last thrown open to the cause of missionary enterprise. But Grant and Simeon had seen that chaplains might go where missionaries could not go, even in the days of the most stringent limitations; chaplains at least had a status in which they could learn the native tongue and translate parts of Scripture without political interference. Therefore Grant set out to teach his colleagues how to look for able chaplains in the ranks of Simeon's disciples, and in 1796 Claudius Buchanan sailed for India, the first of a noble band of unofficial missionaries.

Thus for forty years, from 1796 until his death, Simeon exercised what all knew to be a controlling influence in the choice of chaplains, and he used that long opportunity with rare faith and foresight. Henry Martyn sailed in 1805, Daniel Corrie in 1807, Thomas Thomason in 1808, and Hough, and Dealtry, and a host of others, in the years that ensued. In January 1814 he wrote to Thomason: 'I have always been afraid of urging on any one so important a step as the going to India, lest when they have crossed the line, they should begin to doubt whether God sent them or I....O, that God might thrust them out, and then they will go to some purpose!'[65] But in the next two years he was able to send no less than twelve men to take up posts as chaplains in India![66] In a private memorandum which he wrote in 1829 he made this great statement: 'Almost all the good men who have gone to India these forty years have been recommended by me.'[68] This was a fact which he wished to place on record, in no selfish or boastful spirit, but in humble and thankful surprise. He had good ground for his humorous claim to look on India as his diocese, and when Calcutta was made the seat of a bishopric, to speak of it as his province! In 1830 he came upon the letter of 1787 from Brown and Grant, and on its front he penned one brief remark: 'It merely shows how early God enabled me to act for India; to provide for which has now for forty-two years been a principal and an incessant object of my care and labour.'[69] He was the intimate friend and trusted adviser of Daniel Wilson in the early years of his great episcopate; letters full of wisdom and of courage went to him from Cambridge as long as life allowed. But his last links with that great land were forged in the persons of the missionary, Alexander Duff, whose spiritual ancestry can be traced back to his first tour of Scotland, and the masterly Governor of the North-West, James Thomason, whose education had been placed in his hands in England.

But there was yet another avenue by means of which he strove to serve the whole cause of foreign missions, for the failure of Grant's plan for a State-sponsored mission led him to think in terms of a voluntary society. In May 1795 he was one of a small group of clergy who had met at Rauceby, when the right use of a bequest of £4,000 was discussed. Someone proposed that it should be used for foreign missions, but the matter was shelved until they met again in the autumn. It was then raised in the form of a debate on the wisdom of training men for missionary service in the Church of England; but once again it was deferred in spite of Simeon, who had summed up the pros and cons with that flair for precise statement for which he was renowned. But he could not dismiss it from his mind, and the efforts which he saw put forth in other quarters kept him keen and alert. In 1792 the Baptist Missionary Society had been formed, and William Carey had gone out to Serampore; in 1795 the London Missionary Society had been formed, and The Duff had sailed for the Southern Seas. Therefore he made up his mind to bring the subject before the Eclectic Society, the London rendezvous of men like Venn and Scott and Pratt. In February 1796 he raised the whole question with a speech on one clear issue: 'With what propriety, and in what mode, can a mission be attempted to the heathen from the Established Church?' Thomas Scott and Basil Woodd were the only two of those present who would join hands with him, so strong was the fear of disapproval by Church authorities or of interference with the older Societies. But Scott urged that it would start things stirring, would set up a spirit of prayer, and Woodd lived to declare that this discussion proved to be the foundation of the Church Missionary Society.[70]

The year 1796 saw the formation of the two Scottish missionary societies, so that Simeon's interest in a voluntary society for the Church of England was still kept at white heat. His next step was to bring the whole matter before three great laymen, Charles Grant, Henry Thornton, and William Wilberforce, and there is a notable reference to his eager spirit in the diary kept by Wilberforce: 'Nov. 9th, 1797; Dined and slept at Battersea Rise for missionary meeting. Simeon, Charles Grant, Venn. Something, but not much, done. Simeon in earnest!' Dr Eugene Stock says that this 'dinner at Clapham was more important in the world's history than the Lord Mayor's Banquet at the Guildhall the same evening!'[71] In March 1799 Charles Grant and Simeon were present at a further meeting of the Eclectic, and once more Simeon made a stirring appeal for a practical decision. One month later, on April 12, the sequel appeared, for on that date the Society for Missions to Africa and The East came into being. Simeon became a country member of the first committee, but the distance of Cambridge from London in those days of leisured travel made it impossible for him to take a more active part in its later development as the Church Missionary Society. But he preached the second sermon for the Society at St. Anne's, Blackfriars, in 1802,[72] and he spoke five times at anniversary meetings which were first arranged in 1813.[73] He was made an Honorary Life Governor of the Society,[74] and he gave the valedictory address to sixteen missionaries who were farewelled in 1817.[75] Thus the birth of the Church Missionary Society had been due in no small degree to the parental pains of Simeon, though he would have been the first to agree that the honour was fully shared by Venn and Scott and Pratt. He was unfeignedly thankful as life wore on to see how God had set His seal on that early venture of faith by His blessing in the ends of the earth.

Charles Simeon was a real power for God in the life of Cambridge by the time when the new century began to dawn, and his prestige grew with the years as he carried on his labours almost without interruption. There was one long period, however, when his strength so severely failed that he was forced to relinquish all his activities and to absent himself for some months from Cambridge. Early in 1807, after twenty-five years of intensive ministry, this phase of ill-health set in with a loss of voice so complete that he could only preach with extreme difficulty, and then never more than once a Sunday. He felt 'more like one dead than alive' when he left the pulpit, and a whispered conversation was all that he could sometimes manage.[76] This broken state of health lasted with ups and downs for thirteen years; then in 1819 it passed away, completely and suddenly, with no evident physical explanation at all. He had just reached sixty, the age at which he had thought to retire; but this new accession of strength made him resolve that like Whitefield and Wesley, Romaine and Newton, he would die in harness. But those years of reduced effort had been nevertheless years of constant and fruitful toil. The last flames of parochial controversy had flared up in 1811 and in 1815, after thirty years and more of faithful service. It was this last phase of the long trial which distressed him most of all, for the quarrel spread to his own converts so that he felt wounded in the house of his friends.[77] The last outbreak led to several secessions; but this was a painful necessity, and he learned to bless God that the separation had taken place.[78] Thenceforth his flock prospered with a sweet sense of harmony, and he felt that a new and peculiar unction had come to rest on his ministry.[79] 'When a man's ways please the Lord, He maketh even his enemies to be at peace with him' (Prov. 16: 7).

The worst years of social ostracism in university circles had fallen far behind, and he had won toleration, and then recognition, and in the end veneration as the prince of Cambridge preachers. He had preached in Great St. Mary's both in 1796 and in 1809, and he was yet again chosen as the Select Preacher both in 1811 and in 1815. Vast was the change since his first appearance in Great St. Mary's in 1786; there was now not a more popular man in all Cambridge. 'When he preaches before the University', so one correspondent wrote, 'there is not a Master of a College, nor a Master of Arts, nor a Professor, nor an Undergraduate absent, who can possibly be present.'[80] Students had come to form almost half the congregation which flocked to Holy Trinity,[81] and their numbers seemed to increase from year to year.[82] On November 30, 1818, Simeon wrote:

> As for the gownsmen, never was anything like what they are at this day. I am forced to let them go up into the galleries, which I never suffered before; and notwithstanding that, multitudes of them are forced to stand in the aisles for want of a place to sit down. What thanks can I render to the Lord for a sight of these things?[83]

Meanwhile he was surrounded by a succession of men who were as brilliant in academic achievement as they were splendid in spiritual attainment, men who loved him as sons their father and who served him as men their master. There was Thomas Thomason, fifth Wrangler of 1796, and his curate for twelve years until his Indian call in 1808; there was Thomas Sowerby, first Wrangler of 1798, and his colleague for some three years until his premature death in 1808. There was Preston who helped as his curate from 1808 to 1814; there was Scholefield who served as his colleague from 1813 to 1823.[84] There was Sargent, the early convert and trusted friend who died in 1833 as Rector of Lavington; there was Corrie, the famous chaplain and humble saint who died in 1837 as Bishop of Madras. There were later friends and colleagues like Carus, and Clayton, and a host of others, whose praise is still in all the churches; but there was one above all, the friend and curate of his own heart's desire, Henry Martyn.

All that Henry Venn had been to Simeon in the early years of his ministry, Simeon was in turn to Henry Martyn in the rapid growth of his character. Henry Martyn had found rest and redemption at the feet of Christ in the last year of the century, but he owed the development of his soul to the rich influence of Charles Simeon. The two men found themselves drawn, each to the other, in the bonds of Christ with a great depth and wealth of affection, and the friendship between them was akin to that of the Saviour with the disciple whom He loved. Martyn was a fellow curate with Thomason at Holy Trinity from 1803 till 1805; then he sailed for India as chaplain and an unofficial missionary. His brief but brilliant career, first in India, then in Persia, quickly ran its course, while Simeon cheered his soul with English letters full of the love and tender trust of a friend and father. His last portrait was etched in Calcutta in November 1801 when he was on his way to Persia, and was unpacked at India House in London in October 1812 when he was at death's door in Tocat.[85] Simeon was not to know that his life was even then ebbing away, and he went down, full of eager hope, to see the portrait as soon as it could be unpacked. He was not the kind of man to show his feelings in the presence of strangers, but he had no idea of the disclosure of suffering which those features were to reveal. It was a true likeness of the worn and wasted face of his friend, and he could not restrain himself as he read its story of pain and great distress. 'I was so overpowered by the sight that I could not bear to look upon it,' he wrote, 'but turned away, and went to a distance, covering my face, and in spite of every effort to the contrary, crying aloud with anguish.'[86] He could find no words to express the love he felt as he studied that face; he was not to know that two days later Martyn would pass away into the realms of glory to rest for ever in the presence of God.

For long the sight of that dear face was such a grief to Simeon that he could not bear to let his eyes rest on the portrait for more than a moment or so.[87] But time went far to heal the wound, and the portrait was hung over the fireplace of his dining room. There he would look upon it with peculiar affection, and would say to his friends: 'There! See that blessed man! What an expression of countenance! No one looks at me as he does—he never takes his eyes off me, and seems always to be saying, Be in earnest! Don't trifle! Don't trifle!' Then he would smile, and bow gently to the picture, saying: 'And I won't trifle! I won't trifle!'[88] His friends often heard him speak of Henry Martyn with a kind of rapture as his beloved son, and never without a falter in his voice, or moisture in his eye.[89] In 1825 he went to see Mrs. Henry Sherwood who had known and nursed Martyn nearly twenty years before at Cawnpore. 'The old gentleman', so her diary has it, 'neglected everyone to talk to me of Henry Martyn.'[90] It was Corrie who brought home the news of Abdul Musseeh, the one visible trophy of his preaching to the native population. It was news that led to Simeon's noble statement, so rich in truth and so wise in foresight:

> If Abraham had only one child of promise, and that son too had only one who was beloved of God, was Abraham a dry tree? Neither must we estimate at too low a rate the success of our beloved Martyn; for this one convert may have a progeny which in a few years may be numerous as the sands upon the sea-shore.[91]

In 1816 he spent a few days with Corrie and Sargent in order to go through the papers and the journals which might form the basis for a 'Life' of Martyn. 'Truly it has humbled us all in the dust,' he wrote; '... and I conceive that no book except the Bible will be found to excel this.'[92] A year later, when that book was almost ready, he said: 'It will be such a treat as the world has rarely had.'[93] It was the true tribute of a wise judge as well as a close friend; the book was one in a thousand, and the subject was one in ten thousand.

The troubled waters of Simeon's earlier days had subsided with the unfolding century, and the story of his latter years was calm and peaceful. He was never married, and he refused a large fortune on his brother's death in order to retain his benefice and Fellowship. 'The singular way in which I have been called to my present post', he wrote, 'and its almost incalculable importance, forbid the thought of my now leaving it.'[94] Once he had discovered how great were the opportunities as well as the responsibilities of his work in Cambridge, he made up his mind to live and labour in that field of service to the end of his life. Thus in time he refused all the livings which were within the gift of his College, and one or the other of which most men would have taken as a matter of course. Good livings and large fortune were always within his reach, but they could not tempt him away. 'I should equally refuse anything that the King himself could offer me', he once declared, 'that should necessitate me to give up my present position.'[95] He went on with his work with quiet perseverance, never going out of his way to provoke opposition, but never flinching from a full and faithful declaration of what he knew to be the truth. His stand for the gospel had not lost the offence of the Cross, and it was never pleasant to be nicknamed a 'Sim'; but his purity in motive and his diligence in duty won him at length a formative influence in student circles which has rarely been excelled. He could never forget how much he owed both in churchmanship and in character to the wise and loving friendship of old Henry Venn in the years of trial; and to Ellen Elliott as late as in April 1835 he spoke of his 'love to all who have any blood of the Venns in their veins.'[96] But what Venn had taught him he taught his own generation, and that was to love and believe in the Church of England. Simeon recaptured his own younger Evangelical contemporaries, and made them feel at home within the Church of their fathers.[97]

There was at least one home problem in Church affairs which he tackled with much success, and that was the supply of young men for Holy Orders. In 1767 Henry Venn had founded the Elland Clerical Society, and in 1795 Biddulph the Bristol Clerical Society, to raise money for their education. Wilberforce and the Thorntons had been generous subscribers to both Societies, and a steady trickle of men like Samuel Marsden and Thomas Thomason had gone up to Cambridge.[98] But the demand for such curates grew so strong that Simeon determined to found the London Clerical Education Society, and in 1816 it came into being under trustees like Wilberforce and Babington.[99] Within four years there were some twenty young men in training, and his heart was full of thankfulness.[100] Meanwhile his sermon classes and Friday parties were as strong as ever, and the numbers who found their way into his rooms increased from year to year. A friend so wise and genial, a guide so shrewd and luminous, a man so full of human warmth and common sense, one who lived in the eye of all Cambridge for above fifty years, one who taught so many generations of student life, one who had been put in trust of God to mould so many of the future clergy in mind and heart, Simeon came to occupy a place which was almost unique in the Church of England. 'He saw the disciples of his early days the Governors and Professors of the University in his latter,' wrote Daniel Wilson. 'He was known never to have had but one object, never to have preached but one doctrine. First his friends, then his College, then the University, then the large body of the clergy with whom he had been associated, lastly almost the whole country, understood him. They did not all agree with him; but they understood him.'[101] Lord Macaulay, who took his degree in 1822, looking back from a distance in 1844, told one of his sisters: 'As to Simeon, if you knew what his authority and influence were, and how they extended from Cambridge to the most remote corners of England, you would allow that his real sway in the church was far greater than that of any Primate.'[102]

The brief *Memoir* of his own life which he compiled ends with the year 1813, and the record of a green old age is mainly preserved in the letters and scraps of diary gathered up by Canon Carus. Both the *Memoir* and the *Letters* show that a vast correspondence was no small part of his Cambridge activity; there were copies of some seven thousand letters stored up in his sideboard at the close of his life.[103] 'Seldom surely', wrote Moule, 'has the post been better used than by him in these silent labours of love and wisdom.'[104] We learn from these letters how wide and varied was his interest in a multitude of things beyond the precincts of Cambridge, and not least how great was the part he played in the societies which came into being with the full new tide of Evangelical enthusiasm. It was due to his wise counsel and his energetic action that the Bible Society won its foothold in Cambridge in 1811, and he remained its steady friend throughout the years. But the warmest place in his heart had been reserved for the cause of the Jews, and he was a strenuous advocate on their behalf for many years. The London Society for Promoting Christianity for the Jews had been founded in 1809, but it was so mismanaged in the first five years that all hope for its survival was fast disappearing. It was due to Simeon that it was reorganized at the close of 1814, and an unceasing vigilance for its welfare never left him. Twice, in 1815 and in 1819, it took him to Scotland; twice, in 1818 and in 1823, it took him to Europe. Once he paid a visit to Ireland, and he often travelled through England on its behalf. The recovery of Israel was a prospect very dear to him to the end, and he composed his last testimony to the value of this work for the Jews on his death-bed. But no Society could satisfy his love for individuals, and all his life, in or out of Cambridge, he was a fisher of men and a winner of souls. There were men like Stewart of Moulin, in 1796, or like Konig of Holland, in 1807, whose story was often re-enacted in other lives as the years passed away. He watched for souls, not so much by effort as by habit, and his patience was crowned with rare success.

Meanwhile he saw a grave problem in the exercise of Church Patronage, and in the great difficulty of securing a suitable succession in a parish. Some of the best and most godly men in the Church, like Romaine and Newton, were left unbeneficed for years, while absentee rectors and pluralist clergy held all the most valuable livings without care or concern for souls. And then there was too much cause to fear lest the few Evangelical vicars like Venn should be replaced as Venn had been by some careless worldling; the church bell was ringing for the Thursday evening lecture in Huddersfield when Venn's successor arrived, and his first action was to stop the bell and suppress the service. John and Henry Thornton, father and son, had spent large sums in the purchase of advowsons that they might give them to worthily qualified clergy, and on Henry Thornton's death in 1815 Simeon discovered that he had been named as one of the three trustees for the presentation to these livings. It was only the year before that he had watched by the peaceful death-bed of his brother Edward, and had refused the gift of half his great fortune; but he could not refuse a bequest of, £15,000 for the spread of the gospel, and he resolved to use most of the capital and all the interest for the purchase of the rights of patronage.[105] Thus he inherited the Thornton policy, but he applied it with keener strategy; other friends gave him the money to promote the design on a larger scale, or surrendered to him livings which had been in their gift. This led to the creation of the Simeon Trust in 1817, and it controlled at least twenty-one advowsons by the time of his death.[106] It was thus that he tried to solve the vexed problem for an Evangelical continuity; he bought up key-livings in large towns and cities as spheres of soul-winning service. Very solemn was the charge which he drew up in the Name of God for the Trustees; they were to heed nothing but the glory of God and the fitness of their nominee in each appointment which they were called upon to make.

Simeon was a preacher of no mean fame in an age when preaching was too often defaced by artificial style and monotonous voice. Seldom did his sermons cost him less than twelve hours of study; often he spent more than twice that time on an address.[107] He hammered out his own principles of delivery and exposition, and made them the basis of his sermon classes. His aim was to instruct students in the right exercise of their voice, and in the real character of their work; unity of design and clarity of address were the two great objects which he strove to attain. It is hard for us to realize how novel it was for an English teacher to lay down a programme of this kind in the eighteenth century; for it would contradict the line of tradition which had long ruled the whole concept of the art of preaching, and that, in the very centre of Church life and training. In 1792 he found his own principles embodied in *Claude's Essay on Sermon Composition*,[108] and in 1796 he revised and improved this Essay for publication with an *Appendix of One Hundred Skeleton Sermons*.[109] Perhaps the name he chose was a mistake, but those who had heard him preach knew that he at all events could make the dry bones live! That *Appendix* was the germ of what now became his lifelong literary work, for at various intervals he brought out new sets of sermons to light up the laws of composition. They were like bare backbones, with no waste or trimming; they were simple outlines, full of strength and substance. His complete Works were revised and arranged with the utmost care in 1833, and were published in twenty-one large octavo volumes bearing the title of *Horae Homileticae*. This was the great literary accomplishment of his lifetime, and it contains some two thousand sermons which take us through every important text or passage in the Bible.

His English style was simple and direct, with nothing florid or ornate, and the Skeletons are most suggestive for those who would explain or would enforce the Word of God. To be understood, to reach heart and conscience, was his constant and unmistakable purpose; but the gravity of that purpose and the dignity of his message kept his diction always free from tameness and raised it at times to noble heights of grandeur.[110] But the written outline can give but a faint idea of the power of the spoken message, for he possessed some truly great gifts of action and address. His style of delivery as a young man was earnest and impassioned to a degree; it was still in old age lively and impressive in no common measure.[111] Voice and gesture were marked by the natural and unstudied power of purest sincerity and strongest reality; he could not fail to hold his audience with the unlaboured utterance and the tremendous reverence with which he spoke. The moral force of that preaching, the thrill it sent through mind and soul, filled his church with hearers; Great St. Mary's as well as Trinity was always thronged for his preaching, for indeed, asked Canon Abner Brown, 'who ever heard a dry sermon from Simeon's lips?'[112] His sermons as Select Preacher in 1811 packed the galleries with masters as well as with gownsmen,[113] and in 1815 there was scarce room to move in the tight-wedged mass of people.[114] Twice more did he appear as the Select Preacher, and the result was just the same. In 1823 many could not get in at all,[115] and in 1831 the church was packed with men from all ranks of academic life who were drawn to sit at the feet of the old man eloquent.[116] Canon John Babington said that he heard him for the first time when he went up in 1810, and he went on to add: 'Never before or since have I heard a preacher who seemed so to take me by the hand, and lead me aside into close communion with himself as to the state of my own soul.'[117] And that was the experience of scores who heard through him the Voice of One who hath the words of eternal life.

The English Church can have had few sons and servants more loyal and devoted than Charles Simeon. His early Christian life owed nothing to Church parties, and he always retained a certain air of detached and independent judgment. But while he kept up a receptive attitude to the whole of Revelation, he never moved from the anchorage where his soul had first found its rest. He was an Evangelical by all the persuasion of his own most sacred experience, and his closest friends from first to last were men of the Evangelical School. It was Simeon more than the greatest of all his forerunners who solved the problem of Church discipline, and proved that the warmest Evangelical could and should be loyal to the worship of the Church of England.[118] It was Simeon more than the wisest of all his companions who solved the problem of Church patronage, and proved that the truest Evangelical could and should be loyal to the order of the Church of England.[119] He was a convinced and thoughtful churchman who loved the ancient order and solemn worship of the Prayer Book, and who longed that others should love and venerate it too. He could not bear those who were always spying out the faults of the Church; such faults at the worst were no more than spots on the face of the sun. He deplored the coldness and slackness which prevailed in Church circles, and made it his sacred task to relight the fires of faith and love. One of his great objects in life was to promote 'that comprehensive, and generous, and harmonious, as well as devout spirit, in the Church.'[120] Thus the great Revival of the past century found the solution for its dilemmas in the schools of Cambridge before ever the voice of John Henry Newman had been heard in Oxford, for Charles Simeon trained his men as churchmen at the very outset of their career in a way that was bound to leave its mark throughout the whole Church of England.

But that was not all, for no one ever preached the gospel with more sober good sense than Simeon. This is clearly illustrated by the way in which he pacified and harmonized the cross currents of the Calvinistic controversy which had troubled the whole stream of Evangelical life and unity.[121] It had parted Whitefield from the Wesleys in the hey-day of their labours, and it had widened the whole gap between the Church Evangelicals and the Methodist Movement ever since. The whole controversy was still alive and vigorous in his early manhood, and he could not escape from its problems. On his first encounter with John Wesley, late in 1784, he had accosted the good old veteran with some bluntness: 'Sir, I understand that you are called an Arminian, and I have been sometimes called a Calvinist; and therefore I suppose we are to draw daggers. But before I consent to begin the combat, with your permission, I will ask you a few questions.' Wesley gave his consent, and his replies soon won Simeon completely. 'Sir,' he said, 'with your leave I will put up my dagger again, for this is all my Calvinism…. It is in substance all that I hold, and as I hold it; and therefore if you please…we will cordially unite in those things wherein we agree.'[122] He set out to reduce the whole thing to order, and to view it with a just sense of balance and reserve. He felt that Truth lay not in this extreme nor that extreme, nor yet in the middle; it lay in both extremes, and he would oscillate from one to the other.[123] He was like a man swimming in the Atlantic, and he had no fear lest one hand should beat against Europe and the other against America.[124] He would speak with the same voice of unqualified authority as the inspired penmen of Holy Writ, whether it were on the subject of God's sovereignty or man's responsibility. It was this unswerving adherence to the whole Scriptural conception that helped him to compose the long quarrel with such success.

Charles Simeon was of middle stature, but his upright carriage made him look taller than he was. He held his head erect, almost more than erect, while his aquiline nose and prominent chin were full of personality. He had a singularly bright smile, and his whole aspect spoke of cheerful goodness.[125] There was about him a certain childlike air of unconscious vanity which would sometimes annoy those who did not really know him; but to his friends it only seemed to lend fresh charm to his true and profound humility. The chief weakness in his train of virtue was quickness of temper, and it was not until towards the close of life that this haste was fully subdued.[126] 'There was much fire in his nature', so Moule observed; there was wild fire as well as the fire of sacred passion. And with all his insight into the ways of grace, he does not seem to have seen how that fire could be controlled; he did not see that there is an internal victory which will crush no element of true character, but will bring the whole man into abundant harmony.[127] But his lifelong habits of prayer would go far to subdue all the inborn passions of heat; he would be found one day stricken with penitent grief, and the next day speechless with adoring love.[128] 'I am, I feel I am, a brand plucked out of the burning,' so he wrote with mingled grief and gladness only two years before his death; 'but oh! what dreadful marks of the fire are upon me to this hour!'[129] But his letters all tell of the vigorous intelligence and the vigilant activity of one to whom nothing human could be indifferent, and his infirmities were all absorbed in the majesty of a character which was animated by a simple desire for God's glory. It was the eminent quality of his own masculine character that made his life such a force in Cambridge, and such a power for good throughout the whole Church of England.

From his bedroom a short but steep flight of stairs led to a spacious attic; thence an exit through a glass door opened on to the leads. This gave him an oratory on the roof where no eye save that of his Maker could observe him. Here he would walk beside the stone wall at the edge of the building, or up and down an aisle between two steep ridges on the roof-top.[130] No one ever knew how often that roof was the silent witness to his sighs or his tears as he knelt or trod those leads in prayer and penitence. He once said that he had no wish to write of his own life in the detail of its inner knowledge of God, for the interior working of his heart in the sphere of its spiritual experience was to him most sacred.[131] 'I conceive', he declared in 1817, 'that neither the worst nor the best of any man can be or ought to be known to any but God.'[132] But for forty years, so he could claim in 1819, there were but two objects which he had longed to see: 'The one is my own vileness, and the other is the glory of God in the face of Jesus Christ.... By this I seek to be not only humbled and thankful, but humbled in thankfulness before my God and Saviour continually.'[133] He felt that where humility is not in sight, holiness is at least on the wing, and he laboured with all his soul to win the true spirit of pure humility. 'This is the religion which I love,' he wrote in 1827; 'I love simplicity; I love contrition; I love affiance; I love the tender breathings of affection.'[134] 'I long to be in my proper place,' he wrote in 1832, 'my hand on my mouth, and my mouth in the dust.'[135] It was this deep inner reality of grace that gave him such an air of moral power and dignity. It had fostered his rare gifts of wisdom and candour, and had tempered his best traits of feeling and fervour. His words in a letter to a forlorn friend show what real insight he had into the needs of heart and soul: 'You are nothing, and it discourages you; but you must be content to be nothing, that Christ may be all in all.'[136]

'I seem to be so near the goal that I cannot but run with all my might!'[137] So he wrote in 1828; but a long sunset path still lay before the good old man. In 1832 he kept the jubilee of his appointment to Trinity; in 1833 he had an audience with His Majesty King William IV. His health had been broken from time to time by more or less severe attacks of gout, but he entered upon the last year of his life, the year 1836, as well as he could wish. He at once carried out a five hundred mile tour to visit some of the churches in the gift of his Trust, and he heard while en route that he had been chosen for the eighth time as the Select Preacher. This was no mean honour in view of his great age, and he at once began to draft the four sermons it would entail. His great zeal and vigour seemed to be at full stretch, and he found it hard to realize that he was so close to the eternal world. His last sermon was delivered in Holy Trinity on September 18, and he remarked: 'I preached...with as much energy as ever I did in my life, and with as much comfort to myself.'[138] Three days later he went to call on the new Bishop at Ely, and was received with marked kindness. But the day was damp and chill, and he lingered too long in the Cathedral. The cold, moist air was the direct cause of a sharp illness, and he spent his birthday, on the 24th, in bed. He did make a partial recovery, but a short drive on a raw day brought back the pain and the fever with fresh severity. He now knew that this was just the footfall of death, and he prepared himself with joy for the hour of release. 'What may be my views of eternity when it comes very near, I know not,' he had written twenty long years before; 'but my trust is in the tender mercy of my God in Christ Jesus, and I can joyfully leave myself in His hands.'[139] And so he did.

His heart was at rest in the love of God, and his smile grew brighter and more peaceful as life began to ebb away. He longed to be alone with his closest friends and with God, and nothing could exceed the calm dignity of his demeanour. 'I seem to have nothing to do but to wait,' he said; 'there is now nothing but peace, the sweetest peace.'[140] Words came slowly, with long pauses, often only in clear whispers; and in the last few days he suffered grievously, and his voice was scarcely audible. But faith stood firm. 'Jesus Christ,' he murmured, 'is my all in all.'[141] And thought was clear. 'My principles were not founded on fancies or enthusiasm,' he said; 'but there is a reality in them, and I find them sufficient to support me in death.'[142] On Friday, November 11, with great effort, but not one word, he clasped his hands for the last time in the manner of prayer, and then stretched them out as if in farewell to all his friends. That night William Carus took his withered hand in his own and then slowly voiced the ancient benediction:

> The Lord bless thee, and keep thee;
> the Lord make His face shine upon thee,
>   and be gracious unto thee;
> the Lord lift up His countenance upon thee,
>   and give thee peace.
>
> Num. 6: 24–6

A faint 'Amen' was breathed back in reply, and that was the last word he was heard to articulate. Unconscious, motionless, he lay until near two o'clock on the Sunday afternoon, the hour when the bell of Great St. Mary's began to ring for the service at which he was to have appeared once more as the Select Preacher. But if the sound of that great bell were heard at all in the room where he lay, it must have been like the chime that tolls for the passing of a soul. There was a slight momentary struggle as the bell ceased to toll, and then, on Sunday, November 13, 1836, at the age of 77, he sped away at the peal of the bells in the fields of glory.

Bibliography

William Carus, *Memoirs of the Life of the Rev. Charles Simeon, M.A.* (1847).

Abner William Brown, *Recollections of the Conversation Parties of the Rev. Charles Simeon, M.A.* (1863).

Handley C. G. Moule, *Charles Simeon* ('Leaders of Religion' Series, 1892).

C. H. Simpkinson, 'Charles Simeon', *Chapter X in Typical English Churchmen*, Edited by William Edward Collins (1902).

H. Hensley Henson, *Sibbes and Simeon: An Essay on Patronage* (1932); A Symposium, Centenary Addresses on Charles Simeon (1936).

John MacLeod, 'Charles Simeon', January issue of *The Evangelical Quarterly* (1936).

Charles Smyth, *Simeon and Church Order* (1940).

M. A. C. Warren, Charles Simeon, No. XI in 'Great Churchmen' Series (1950).

John Venn and Henry Venn, *The Life and a Selection from the Letters of the Late Rev. Henry Venn, M.A.* (1837).

Edwin Sidney, *The Life of the Rev. Rowland Hill, A.M.* (1834).

Margaret Seeley, *The Later Evangelical Fathers* (1913).

James Stephen, *Essays in Ecclesiastical Biography* (New Ed., 1875)

Eugene Stock, *The History of The Church Missionary Society* (1899).

Handley C. G. Moule, *The Evangelical School in the Church of England* (1901).

G. R. Balleine, *A History of the Evangelical Party* (New Ed., 1933).

Endnotes

Chapter 1 - William Grimshaw

1 Newton, *Memoirs of Grimshaw*, 6.
2 Ryle, *Christian Leaders*, 111.
3 Ryle, 111.
4 John Wesley, *Journals*, Vol. IV, 494; Newton, 94.
5 Ryle, 111.
6 Newton, 50.
7 Mrs. Gaskell, *Charlotte Bronte*, 23.
8 Newton, 100.
9 Balleine, 65.
10 Balleine, 66.
11 Cragg, *Grimshaw*, 24.
12 Ryle, 143.
13 Cragg, 22.
14 Newton, 142–3.
15 Newton, 112–13.
16 Newton, 120–22.
17 F. J. Powicke, *A Life of The Reverend Richard Baxter*, 45.
18 Ryle, 140 n.
19 Newton, 110.
20 Newton, 109.
21 Newton, 144.
22 Cragg, 97.
23 Ryle, 117.
24 Newton, 63.
25 Newton, 109.
26 Balleine, 67–8.
27 Tyerman, *John Wesley*, Vol. II, 13.
28 Newton, 65.
29 G. Elsie Harrison, Son to Susanna, 350; cf. *Wuthering Heights*, "Und t'sahnd uh't Gospel still i' yer lugs", 18.
30 Newton, 69.
31 Cragg, 22.
32 Cragg, 22.
33 Cragg, 57–8.
34 Newton, 151.
35 Cragg, 23.
36 Cragg, 22.
37 Cragg, 42.
38 Ryle, 129.

39 Cragg, 47.
40 Ryle, 130.
41 Tyerman, John Wesley, Vol. I, 536.
42 Op. Cit., 536.
43 Cragg, 42.
44 Ryle, 115.
45 Cragg, 25.
46 *Lady Huntingdon*, Vol. II, 314.
47 Cragg, 37, 38.
48 Overton and Relton, 149.
49 Cragg, 11.
50 Newton, 59.
51 Cragg, 47.
52 Cragg, 105.
53 Ryle, 127.
54 Ryle, 127–8.
55 John Wesley, *Letters*, Vol. III, 30.
56 Cragg, 64.
57 *Lady Huntingdon*, Vol. I, 259.
58 Op. cit., 14.
59 Alfred Lord Tennyson, *Lady Clara Vere de Pere*, VII, lines 7–8.
60 Charles Wesley, *Journals*, Vol. I, 432, 440.
61 John Wesley, *Journals*, Vol. III, 293.
62 Cragg, 42.
63 John Wesley, *Journals*, Vol. III, 369.
64 Cragg, 46.
65 John Wesley, *Journals*, Vol. IV, 67 n.
66 Op. cit., 68.
67 Op. cit., 114.
68 Charles Wesley, *Journals*, Vol. II, 227.
69 Op. Cit., 129.
70 John Wesley, *Journals*, Vol. IV, 212, 213.
71 Op. cit., 310.
72 Op. cit., 332–3.
73 Op. cit., 447.
74 Op. cit., 468–9.
75 Wesley, *Letters*, Vol. IV, 160.
76 Tyerman, *Whitefield*, Vol. II, 234.
77 *Lady Huntingdon*, Vol. I, 265–6.
78 Op. Cit., 156.
79 Op. cit., 156.
80 Tyerman, *Whitefield*, Vol. II, 285.
81 Op. cit., 315.
82 Cragg, 46; cf. Whitefield, Works, Vol. III, Letter DCCCXCI, 29.
83 *Lady Huntingdon*, Vol. I, 267.
84 Whitefield, *Works*, Vol. III, Letter MCXLIX, 190.
85 Tyerman, *Whitefield*, Vol. II, 381.
86 *Lady Huntingdon*, Vol. I, 255; cf. Cragg, 75–82.
87 Tyerman, *Wesley*, Vol. I, 536.
88 Tyerman, *Wesley*, Vol. II, 16.
89 *Lady Huntingdon*, Vol. I, 261.
90 Op. Cit., 260, 261.
91 Wesley, *Letters*, Vol. II, 153–6.
92 *Lady Huntingdon*, Vol. I, 259, 260.
93 Tyerman, *John Wesley*, Vol. II, 17.
94 Op. cit., 17–18.
95 Newton, 62; cf. *Lady Huntingdon*, Vol. I, 261 n.
96 Cragg, 46.
97 Cragg, 95.
98 Newton, 71.
99 Newton, 120.
100 Tyerman, *Wesley's Designated Successor*, 384.
101 Cragg, 97.
102 Ryle, 147.
103 Ryle, 119.
104 Cragg, 43.
105 Newton, 100, 101.

106 Newton, 102.

107 Ryle, 147.

108 Cragg, 45.

109 Tyerman, *Wesley*, Vol. II, 204.

110 Op. cit., 385.

111 Op. cit., 387.

112 Newton, 106, 107.

113 Wesley, *Journals*, Vol. VI, 229.

114 *Lady Huntingdon*, Vol. I, 274.

115 Ryle, 147.

116 Bull, *Newton*, 96.

117 Bull, *Newton*, 107.

118 Newton, 154–5.

119 Ryle, 147.

120 Venn, *Life and Letters*, 277.

121 Wesley, *Journals*, Vol. IV, 495.

122 Op. cit., Vol. III, 422; cf. Charles Wesley, *Journals*, Vol. II, 67.

123 *Lady Huntingdon*, Vol. I, 283.

124 Cragg, 90.

125 Mrs. Gaskell, 24.

126 Newton, 141.

127 Cragg, 62.

128 Cragg, 67.

129 Newton, 97.

130 Cragg, 61.

131 Ryle, 139.

132 Ryle, 118.

133 *Lady Huntingdon*, Vol. I, 284.

134 Tyerman, *Whitefeld*, Vol. II, 464.

135 Thomas Haweis, *The Life of William Romaine*, 108.

136 *Lady Huntingdon*, Vol. I, 285, 286.

137 Cragg, 104.

138 Cragg, 90.

139 Newton, 186; cf. *Lady Huntingdon*, Vol. I, 286 n.

Chapter 2 - John Berridge

1 Whittingham, 2.

2 Whittingham, 19–20.

3 Tyerman, *Whitefield*, Vol. II, 441.

4 Whittingham, 5.

5 Ryle, 221.

6 Smyth, 159.

7 Whittingham, 6.

8 Ryle, 222.

9 Berridge, *Works*, 350,

10 Op. cit., 350.

11 Op. cit., 351.

12 Whittingham, 10,

13 Whittingham, 11.

14 Berridge, *Works*, 357.

15 Whittingham, 22.

16 Smyth, 163.

17 Smyth, 163, 164.

18 Smyth, 164.

19 Whittingham, 13.

20 Whitefield, *Works*, Vol. III, Letter MCCVII, 238.

21 Whittingham, 13; cf. Smyth, 165.

22 Wesley, *Journals*, Vol. IV, 291.

23 Wesley, *Journals*, Vol. IV, 300.

24 Wesley, *Letters*, Vol. IV, 58.

25 Whittingham, 50.

26 Wesley, *Journals*, Vol. IV, 318.

27 Op. cit., 318.

28 Op. cit., 319.

29 Op. cit., 320.

30 Andrew Bonar, *Memoir of Robert Murray M'Cheyne*, 547–8.

31 Whittingham, 51.

32 *Lady Huntingdon*, Vol. I, 368.

33 Whittingham, 28.

34 Whittingham, 32.
35 Wesley, Journals, Vol. IV, 336.
36 Op. cit., 338.
37 Op. cit., 340–41.
38 Op. cit., 341.
39 Op. cit., 342.
40 Op. cit., 344–7.
41 Op. cit., 349–50.
42 Op. cit., 359.
43 Tyerman, *Wesley's Designated Successor*, 51–2.
44 *Lady Huntingdon*, Vol. I, 399–400.
45 Berridge, *Works*, 394.
46 Op. cit., 475–6.
47 Smyth, 258 n.
48 Berridge, *Works*, 476.
49 Smyth, 261.
50 Berridge, *Works*, 516.
51 Smyth, 266–7; cf. Berridge, *Works*, 59.
52 Smyth, 250.
53 Berridge, *Works*, 517.
54 Abner Brown, *Conversation Parties*, 200.
55 Abner Brown, *Conversation Parties*, 200.
56 Whittingham, 33.
57 Berridge, *Works*, 532.
58 Op. cit., 523.
59 Op. cit., 533.
60 Abner Brown, *Conversation Parties*, 200.
61 Op. Cit., 202.
62 Berridge, *Works*, 72–3.
63 Berridge, *Works*, 73–5.
64 Whittingham, 20.
65 Berridge, *Works*, 358–9.
66 Wesley, *Letters*, Vol. IV, 92–3.
67 Wesley, *Journals*, Vol. IV, 360.
68 Smyth, 177.
69 Whittingham, 59.
70 Sidney, Rowland Hill, 21.
71 Op. cit., 43.
72 Op. cit., 50.
73 Op. cit., 50.
74 Op. cit., 57–8.
75 Op. cit., 91.
76 Op. cit., 92.
77 Op. cit., 173, 174.
78 Wesley, *Journals*, Vol. IV, 433, 483.
79 Whitefield, *Works*, Vol. III, Letter MCCXLII, 264; Letter MCCXLV, 265 postscript.
80 Smyth, 187.
81 Whittingham, 14–17.
82 Berridge, *Works*, 313.
83 Wesley, *Letters*, Vol. IV, 206.
84 Berridge, *Works*, 327.
85 Op. Cit., 187.
86 Op. Cit., 189.
87 Op. Cit., 190.
88 Op. cit., 194.
89 Op. cit., 195.
90 Op. cit., 200.
91 Op. Cit., 221.
92 Op. cit., 316–17.
93 Op. cit. p., 384.
94 Op. cit., 387.
95 Tyerman, *Wesley's Designated Successor*, 297.
96 Op. cit., 298.
97 Whittingham, 17.
98 Whittingham, 18.
99 Whittingham, 61.
100 Tyerman, *Wesley's Designated Successor*, 172.
101 Op. cit., 371.
102 Whittingham, 61–3.
103 Abner Brown, *Conversation Parties*, 201, 202.
104 Berridge, *Works*, 123.
105 Ryle, 238.
106 Balleine, 99.
107 Smyth, 182.
108 Whittingham, 30.
109 Whittingham, 31, 32.

110 Whittingham, 34.
111 Whittingham, 34; cf. Smyth, 267 n.
112 William Romaine, *Works*, 710–11.
113 Berridge, *Works*, 366.
114 Op. cit., 386, 395, 399, 401, 406–7.
115 Ryle, 216.
116 Ryle, 236.
117 Berridge, *Works*, 526–7.
118 *Lady Huntingdon*, Vol. I, 358.
119 Whittingham, 21; cf. Wesley, *Journals*, Vol. IV, 342.
120 Berridge, *Works*, 508–9.
121 Op. cit., 508.
122 Tyerman, *Whitefield*, Vol. II, 427.
123 Op. cit., 539.
124 *Lady Huntingdon*, Vol. I, 323.
125 Op. cit., Vol. II, 19.
126 Op. cit., Vol. I, 366.
127 Op. cit., Vol. II, 20.
128 Berridge, *Works*, 515.
129 Op. cit., 79.
130 Venn, 191.
131 Venn, 206.
132 Berridge, *Works*, 394.
133 Venn, 233.
134 Berridge, *Works*, 402.
135 Op. cit., 404.
136 Op. cit., 513.

137 Op. cit., 418.
138 Berridge, *Works*, 445–6.
139 Smyth, 279–81.
140 Abner Brown, *Conversation Parties*, 201.
141 Venn, 518.
142 Sidney, *Rowland Hill*, 161–2.
143 Berridge, *Works*, 491.
144 Balleine, 101.
145 Berridge, *Works*, 368.
146 Op. cit., 502.
147 Ryle, 246.
148 Whittingham, 38.
149 Berridge, *Works*, 160.
150 Op. cit., 119–121.
151 Op. cit., 520.
152 Op. cit., 530.
153 Op. cit., 512.
154 Venn, 191.
155 Berridge, *Works*, 531.
156 Venn, 233.
157 Berridge, *Works*, 413.
158 Venn, 354.
159 Berridge, *Works*, 447.
160 Op. cit., 448.
161 Op. cit., 457.
162 Op. cit., 458.
163 Venn, 501.
164 Berridge, *Works*, 470.
165 Whittingham, 43.
166 Venn, 519.

Chapter 3 - Henry Venn

1 *Annals*, 50; cf. Charles Wesley, *Journals*, Vol. I, 138.
2 Venn, *Life and Letters*, 6.
3 Op. cit., 6.
4 *Annals*, 68 n.
5 Venn, *Life and Letters*, 15.
6 Op. cit., 13, 14.
7 Op. cit., 247.

8 Op. cit., 21.
9 Op. cit., 188.
10 *The Oxford Methodists*, 348; cf. *Life of Wesley*, Vol. II, 186.
11 Haweis, *Life of Romaine*, 209; cf. *Lady Huntingdon*, Vol. I, 224.
12 *Lady Huntingdon*, Vol. I, 223.

13 Op. cit., 223.

14 Venn, *Life and Letters*, 152.

15 *Lady Huntingdon*, Vol. I, 219;
cf. Whitefield, *Works*, Vol. III,
Letter MCXCIV p. 228.

16 *Lady Huntingdon*, Vol. I, 225.

17 *Lady Huntingdon*, Vol. I, 225.

18 Op. cit., 430.

19 Balleine, 56.

20 *Lady Huntingdon*, Vol. I, 228.

21 Op. cit., 396–7.

22 Venn, *Life and Letters*, 159, 160.

23 *Annals*, 79.

24 Wesley, *Journals*, Vol. IV, 210.

25 Op. cit., 333.

26 Knight, 37.

27 Venn, *Life and Letters*, 77.

28 Op. cit., 45.

29 Op. cit., 79.

30 *Lady Huntingdon*, Vol. I, 282.

31 Venn, *Life and Letters*, 128.

32 *Annals*, 82.

33 Venn, *Life and Letters*, 145.

34 Venn, *Life and Letters*, 82.

35 Op. cit., 85.

36 *Complete Duty of Man*, xxxiii.

37 Sir James Stephen, 444.

38 Ryle, 290.

39 *Lady Huntingdon*, Vol. I, 399-
400.

40 Bull, 112.

41 *Lady Huntingdon*, Vol. I, 314,
319.

42 Op. cit., 281.

43 Op. Cit., Vol. II, 124.

44 Op. cit., Vol. I, 477 n.

45 Bull, 153.

46 Venn, *Life and Letters*, 122.

47 *Lady Huntingdon*, Vol. I, 291.

48 Op. Cit., Vol. II, 127.

49 Venn, *Life and Letters*, 153.

50 Op. Cit., 158.

51 Op. cit., 277.

52 Op. cit., 376.

53 Tyerman, *Wesley's Designated
Successor*, 371.

54 Op. cit., 393.

55 Venn, *Life and Letters*, 582.

56 Wesley, *Journals*, Vol. IV, 471.

57 Op. cit., Vol. V, 81–2.

58 Op. cit., Vol. VI, 133-

59 Venn, *Life and Letters*, 362.

60 Venn, *Life and Letters*, 191.

61 Op. cit., 354.

62 Bull, 118; cf: pp. 107, 111.

63 Bull, 153.

64 Venn, *Life and Letters*, 265.

65 Ryle, 277.

66 *Annals*, 106.

67 *Lady Huntingdon*, Vol. I, 291,

68 Op. cit., 300.

69 Venn, *Life and Letters*, 131.

70 Ryle, 287.

71 Venn, *Life and Letters*, 116.

72 Op. cit., 43.

73 Op. cit., 48.

74 *Annals*, 87.

75 Venn, *Life and Letters*, 91.

76 Op. cit., 123, 168.

77 Op. cit., 187.

78 Op. cit., 169.

79 Ryle, 280.

80 Venn, *Life and Letters*, 165.

81 *Annals*, 100.

82 Whittingham, *Works of
Berridge*, 523.

83 Venn, *Life and Letters*, 182.

84 Op. cit., 186; cf. Bull, *John
Newton*, 175.

85 Op. cit., 199.

86 Op. cit., 212.

87 Moule, 26.

88 Wesley, *Journals*, Vol. VI, 52.

89 *Lady Huntingdon*, Vol. II, 57.

90 Op. cit.; pp. 402, 414.

91 Venn, *Life and Letters*, 232.

92 Op. Cit., 238.

93 Op. cit., 317.

94 *Lady Huntingdon*, Vol. II, 321–2.
95 Venn, *Life and Letters*, 329.
96 Op. cit., 374.
97 Op. cit., 400.
98 Op. cit., 415.
99 Op. cit., 194.
100 Op. cit., 199.
101 *Lady Huntingdon*, Vol. I, 479.
102 *Annals*, 120.
103 William Carus, 23.
104 *Annals*, 1181.
105 Venn, *Life and Letters*, 359.
106 Op. cit., 382.
107 Op. cit., 415.
108 Sidney, *Rowland Hill*, 159–61.
109 Venn, *Life and Letters*, 463.
110 Op. cit., 480.
111 Op. cit., 488.
112 Op. cit., 56.
113 Op. cit., 256.
114 Ryle, 291.
115 Bateman, *Daniel Wilson*, Vol. II, 367.
116 Ryle, 295.
117 Venn, *Life and Letters*, 114.
118 Op. cit., 324.
119 Op. cit., 375, 382.
120 Op. cit., 423.
121 Op. cit., 524.
122 Op. cit., 548.
123 Ryle, 298.
124 Venn, *Life and Letters*, 174.
125 Op. cit., 333.
126 Ryle, 292.
127 Venn, *Life and Letters*, 33.
128 Op. cit., 192.
129 Op. cit., 33.
130 Op. cit., 208.
131 Op. cit., 474.
132 Op. cit., 532.
133 Ryle, 298.
134 Samuel Wilberforce, *Life of Wilberforce*, 121 (one vol. ed.).
135 Venn, *Life and Letters*, 527.
136 Eugene Stock, Vol. I, 67.
137 Knight, 300.
138 Knight, 134.
139 Knight, 268.
140 Knight, 124.
141 Venn, *Life and Letters*, 120.
142 Op. cit., 321.
143 Op. cit., 155.
144 Bateman, *Life of Wilson*, Vol. II, 367.
145 Sir James Stephen, 444.
146 Sir James Stephen, 443.
147 Sir James Stephen, 444.
148 Venn, Life and Letters, 211.
149 Op. cit., 251.
150 Op. cit., 56.
151 Op. cit., 299.
152 Op. cit., 422.
153 Op. cit., 428.
154 Op. cit., 435.
155 Op. cit., 485.
156 Op. cit., 483.
157 Op. cit., 493.
158 Op. cit., 498; cf. Bull, 310.
159 Op. cit., 148 n.
160 Op. cit., 510.
161 Op. cit., 528.
162 Op. cit., 530.
163 Haweis, *Life of Romaine*, 210.
164 Bateman, *Life of Wilson*, Vol. II, 367.
165 Venn, *Life and Letters*, 531.
166 Carus, *Life of Simeon*, 104.
167 Venn, *Life and Letters,* 523.
168 Op. cit., 59.

Chapter 4 - Charles Simeon

1 Carus, *Memoirs of Simeon*, 6.
2 Carus, 9.
3 Carus, 232, 518, 654, 711.
4 Moule, 16–17.
5 Carus, 21.
6 Henry Venn, 352.
7 Whittingham, *The Works of John Berridge*, 418.
8 Carus, 41.
9 Carus, 22.
10 Henry Venn, 351.
11 Carus, 23.
12 Carus, 23.
13 Henry Venn, 352.
14 Henry Venn, 352.
15 Moule, 45.
16 Carus, 554.
17 Carus, 713.
18 Carus, 44.
19 Henry Venn, 359.
20 Henry Venn, 359.
21 Henry Venn, 382.
22 Sidney, *Rowland Hill*, 159.
23 John Wesley, *Journals*, Vol. VII, 39; 337–8.
24 Moule, 42.
25 Moule, 44.
26 Carus, 59.
27 Moule, 72.
28 Carus, 605.
29 Moule, 63.
30 Balleine, 130.
31 Carus, 88.
32 Simpkinson, 267.
33 Carus, 92, 93.
34 Carus, 724.
35 Smyth, 281.
36 Carus, 69.
37 Sidney, *Rowland Hill*, 161.
38 Carus, 73.
39 Smyth, 48.
40 Carus, 68.
41 Henry Venn, 480.
42 Carus, 67.
43 Moule, 83.
44 Carus, 307.
45 Carus, 528.
46 Carus, 10.
47 Carus, 114.
48 Carus, 703.
49 Carus, 676 n.
50 Carus, 65.
51 Carus, 85.
52 Carus, 65.
53 Moule, 47.
54 Carus, 46.
55 Carus, 98.
56 Abner Brown, 200–2.
57 Henry Venn, 519.
58 Carus, 555.
59 Carus, 220.
60 Carus, 70.
61 F. W. B. Bullock, *The History of Ridley Hall*, Vol. I, 44, 45.
62 Carus, 271.
63 Balleine, p. 130.
64 Simpkinson, p.261.
65 Carus, 380.
66 Carus, 428.
67 Moule p. 129.
69 Carus, 75.
70 Carus, 111.
71 Eugene Stock, C.M.S., Vol. I, 62, 63.
72 Op. cit., 76, 78.
73 Op. cit., 113, 262.
74 Op. cit., 242.
75 Op. cit., 115.
76 Carus, 538.
77 Carus, 339.

78 Carus, 424.

79 Carus, 495.

80 Smyth, 132 n.

81 Carus, 445.

82 Carus, 471.

83 Carus, 496; cf pp. 550, 593.

84 F. W. B. Bullock, *The History of Ridley Hall*, Vol. I, 49, 50.

85 Henry Martyn, *Journals and Letters*, Vol. II, 324.

86 Carus, 358.

87 Carus, 390.

88 Carus, 391 n.

89 Moule, 233.

90 *The Life and Times of Mrs. Sherwood*, 456.

91 Carus, 390.

92 Carus, 435.

93 Carus, 444.

94 Carus, 231.

95 Carus, 435.

96 Carus, 758.

97 Smyth, 250, 311.

98 Smyth, 243–4.

99 Carus, 432.

100 Carus, 536.

101 Carus, 840.

102 G. O. Trevelyan, *The Life and Letters of Lord Macaulay*, 50 n. [Silver Library, one vol. ed., 1908].

103 Carus, 639.

104 Moule, 181.

105 Carus, 590.

106 Smyth, 246, 247.

107 Carus, 841.

108 Carus, 642.

109 Carus, 143.

110 Moule, 91.

111 Carus, 63.

112 Abner Brown, 10.

113 Carus, 318.

114 Carus, 416.

115 Carus, 589.

116 Carus, 838.

117 Moule, 178.

118 Moule, *The Evangelical School in the Church of England*, 12.

119 Smyth, 283–4.

120 Carus, 534.

121 Moule, *The Evangelical School in the Church of England*, 12.

122 Moule, 100–101.

123 Carus, 600.

124 Carus, 842.

125 Moule, 258.

126 Carus, 823.

127 Moule, 230.

128 Carus, 100, 101.

129 Carus, 735.

130 Carus, 355.

131 Carus, 341.

132 Carus, 450.

133 Carus, 519–20.

134 Carus, 615.

135 Carus, 695.

136 Carus, 734.

137 Carus, 620.

138 Carus, 822.

139 Carus, 437.

140 Carus, 823.

141 Carus, 824.

142 Carus, 824.

Sir Marcus Loane

OXFORD
and the
EVANGELICAL
SUCCESSION

George Whitefield
John Newton
Thomas Scott
Richard Cecil
Daniel Wilson

Oxford and the Evangelical Succession

Sir Marcus Loane

These are the stories of five key ministers of the 18th and 19th centuries who changed the whole spirit of the Church of England – and whose influence is still seen today.

People today are frantically searching for security and are increasingly not finding it in a material philosophy where we are dictated to by other people. A church that hopes to transform this society needs to look to those who were enabled to perform the same task in a similar era.

Each one of these men was associated with Oxford whilst proving their mettle as spiritual leaders. Each one kept alive and added to the passionate flame of a remarkable line of influential church leaders.

No lesser authority than J.C. Ryle placed George Whitefield (1714-1770) as the foremost Christian leader of the 18th century. He, in turn, passed the torch to John Newton (1725-1807). Newton was as a spiritual father to Thomas Scott (1747-1821) and Richard Cecil (1748-1810) and they in turn were the spiritual guides to Daniel Wilson (1778-1858). Wilson launched a missionary emphasis still seen today in Oxford churches.

What this book helps us understand is that the situation that prevailed when these men influenced their society is similar to that of today. If we want to change the world then their stories could inspire us to do just that.

Sir Marcus Loane was the first Australian Archbishop of Sydney and Primate of the Anglican Church of Australia. He was also Principal of Moore Theological College in Sydney. He has written many acclaimed biographical works. His current occupation is as 'an active nonagerian'.

ISBN 978-1-84550-245-4

HISTORY [HM] MAKERS

THE CAMBRIDGE SEVEN

THE TRUE STORY OF ORDINARY MEN USED IN NO ORDINARY WAY

John Pollock

The Cambridge Seven

The true story of ordinary men used in no ordinary way

John Pollock

"It is not surprising that out of the whole-hearted devotion of these seven young men with their "intolerance of shoddy spirituality in themselves or in others, "there should emerge even beyond their huge labours in China, some extraordinary consequences"

Michael Cassidy

Harold Schofield, a brilliant Oxford doctor who had laboured as a missionary in China for many years, was on his knees praying, 'Lord, give me missionaries from British Universities to help in China'.

The day he died, D. E. Hoste applied to Hudson Taylor for mission work in the China Inland Mission (Now Overseas Missionary Fellowship). Schofield's prayer was answered as seven Cambridge students volunteered to leave behind cosy lives of wealth and privilege to serve God in whatever way they were led.

These seven inspired thousands of others to think seriously of missionary service. Included among them was C.T. Studd, captain of England and the finest cricketer of his day – if he could give all that up, then so could anyone!

The story of these seven are an inspiration that God can take people and use them in incredible ways – if they are willing to serve.

As Pollock says in his book 'Theirs is the story of ordinary men, and thus may be repeated'. Will it be repeated in your life?

John Pollock is acknowledged as one of Britain's finest biographers. A Biography prize is awarded in his name by Samford University, Alabama each year.

ISBN 978-1-84550-177-8

"We urgently need a new generation of Simeons"
JOHN STOTT

CHARLES SIMEON

Pastor of a generation

Handley Moule

Charles Simeon

Pastor of a generation

Handley Moule

Charles Simeon (1759-1836) left an indelible impression upon his generation. Educated at Eton and then King's College, Cambridge, he was ordained before he was twenty three.

He was the minister of Holy Trinity Church, Cambridge, for fifty four years, but his appointment met witth opposition from his parishioners which continued unabated for the first ten years. He came through it to be regarded as a great preacher, learned teacher and guide, philanthropist and discipler of young men attempting to enter the ministry.

He became the object of great personal respect and of very wide influence in the church at the time. It is possible that the English church never had a more loving and devoted son and servant than Charles Simeon

'We urgently need a new generation of Simeons'

John Stott

'Simeon's honesty and passion for Christ, his dedication as a Pastor and his sincerity and fire for the truth of the Gospel, shine from this book.'

J R, CLC Book Reviews

'The reading of this book can do nothing but good for Christians today.'

John Diggle, Clay Cross

Handley Moule was Bishop of Durham from 1901-1920. Previously, he was a Professor of Divinity at the University of Cambridge. He was also one of the speakers at the first Keswick Convention.

ISBN 1-85792-310-3
ISBN 978-1-85792-310-1

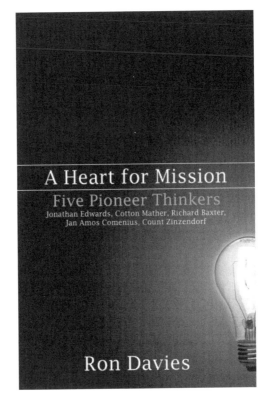

A Heart for Mission

Five Pioneer Thinkers

Jonathan Edwards, Cotton Mather, Richard Baxter,
Jan Amos Comenius, Count Zinzendorf

Ron Davies

A Heart for Mission

Five Pioneer Thinkers

Ron Davies

Jonathan Edwards, Jan Amos Comenius,
Count Zinzendorf, Cotton Mather, Richard Baxter

Many commentators agree that the Protestant Missionary effort really got under way in the late 18th century with the formation of the Baptist Missionary Society. Bearing in mind that the Reformation began in the early 16th Century the obvious question that arises is *'Why did it take Protestants nearly three centuries to act on Jesus' Great Commission mandate?'*

This book goes some of the way to explaining why. We are introduced to five Protestant, Christian thinkers who had a mind for mission, long before the Protestant world as a whole became aware of the need. From the celebrated Jonathan Edwards to the comparatively unknown Jan Amos Comenius, we see how these five men were ahead of their time. They influenced thinking about mission and their comments ultimately led to the missionary explosion which began at the end of the 18th century and which carries on to the present day.

'For those who like to probe beneath the surface of missionary myths – read this fascinating book and be enriched, challenged and inspired.'

Chris Wright, Langham Partnership International

Ron Davies has been thinking about mission for over 40 years. He has lectured at All Nations Christian College since 1964 and has been a visiting lecturer at several Seminaries in Eastern Europe and elsewhere.

ISBN 1-85792-233-6
ISBN 978-1-85792-233-2

GOODCHRISTIANS
GOODHUSBANDS?

Leaving a Legacy in Marriage & Ministry

Doreen Moore

Lessons from the marriages & ministries of
Elizabeth & George Whitefield
Sarah & Jonathan Edwards
Molly & John Wesley

Good Christians, Good Husbands?

Leaving a Legacy in Marriage and Ministry

Doreen Moore

This is the inspiring and convicting account of three eighteenth-century Christian leaders (John Wesley, George Whitfield & Jonathan Edwards), all of whom were passionate about glorifying God by serving Him in their generation. They left an enduring and fruitful legacy through their labours, and they were also married. How they balanced (or did not balance) their passion for ministry with being married is the subject of this book.

This book tells more than just the story of three couples it gives us contemporary lessons too, offering Biblical guidelines and counsel from modern day Christian leaders. Many couples today struggle with how God views the relationship between family and ministry. This book gleans insights from these examples and gives biblical guidelines and counsel from some modern day Christian leaders too.

Resourced by thorough research into the marriages of Wesley, Whitefield and Edwards, this is a truly wise book on the problem of combining ministry and marriage to the glory of God and the good of all concerned.

J. I. Packer

Doreen Moore is a graduate of Trinity Evangelical Divinity School. She lives in Austin, Texas with her husband Dave, and 2 sons. Prior to seminary, Doreen and her husband were on the staff with Campus Crusade for Christ.

ISBN 1-85792-450-9
ISBN 978-1-85792-450-3

Christian Focus Publications

publishes books for all ages

Our mission statement –

STAYING FAITHFUL

In dependence upon God we seek to help make His infallible Word, the Bible, relevant. Our aim is to ensure that the Lord Jesus Christ is presented as the only hope to obtain forgiveness of sin, live a useful life and look forward to heaven with Him.

REACHING OUT

Christ's last command requires us to reach out to our world with His gospel. We seek to help fulfil that by publishing books that point people towards Jesus and help them develop a Christ-like maturity. We aim to equip all levels of readers for life, work, ministry and mission.

Books in our adult range are published in three imprints.

Christian Focus contains popular works including biographies, commentaries, basic doctrine and Christian living. Our children's books are also published in this imprint.

Mentor focuses on books written at a level suitable for Bible College and seminary students, pastors, and other serious readers. The imprint includes commentaries, doctrinal studies, examination of current issues and church history.

Christian Heritage contains classic writings from the past.

Christian Focus Publications Ltd,
Geanies House, Fearn, Ross-shire,
IV20 1TW, Scotland, United Kingdom
info@christianfocus.com
www.christianfocus.com